Radical Islamic Terrorism
In America Today

by RJ Parker
and
Dr. Peter Vronsky

1

Radical Islamic Terrorism
In America Today

by RJ Parker
and
Dr. Peter Vronsky

ISBN-13:978 1523388592
ISBN-10: 1523388595

Copyright and Published (05.2016)

by

VP Publications, an Imprint of

RJ Parker Publishing, Inc.

Published in Canada

Copyrights

This is a work of nonfiction. No names have been changed, no characters invented, no events fabricated.

Table of Contents

This is a work of nonfiction. No names have been changed, no characters invented, no events fabricated.

Quotes

"I refuse to describe the Islamic State and Al Qaeda as groups fueled by "radical Islam" because the term grants them a religious legitimacy they don't deserve. We are not at war with Islam. We are at war with people who have perverted Islam."
-- **President Barack Obama, Feb 18, 2015**

"Let's be clear: Islam is not our adversary. Muslims are peaceful and tolerant people and have nothing whatsoever to do with terrorism."
-- **Hillary Clinton, Nov 19, 2015**

"It is obvious to anybody the hatred [among Muslims] is beyond comprehension. Where this hatred comes from and why, we will have to determine. Until we are able to determine and understand this problem and the dangerous threat it poses, our country cannot be the victims of horrendous attacks by people that believe only in jihad, and have no sense of reason or respect for human life."
-- **Donald Trump, Dec 7, 2015**

Introduction: Four Reasons Why They Hate Us: A Politically Incorrect True History of Islamist Terrorism

by Peter Vronsky, PhD

As this is being written, a Republican candidate for the U.S. Presidency is currently calling on a complete and total ban on Muslims entering the United States until "we figure out what the hell is going on." If we haven't figured out what the hell is going on by now, there is little hope for us. Here is what the hell is going on:

There are basically three categories of Islamist terrorists threatening America today.

First, the two major overseas groups: Al-Qaeda founded twenty-five years ago by Osama bin Laden to fight the Russians in Afghanistan and currently (at this writing) led by Egyptian militant Ayman al-Zawahiri; and its rival, the newly founded IS (Islamic State) also referred to as ISIS/ISIL led by Iraqi militant Abu Bakr al-

Baghdadi.

These two big groups dominate the Islamic extremist movement but are currently turning on each other as rivals, and perhaps if we leave them alone to it, they will destroy each other and we can all go in peace. The emerging conflict between Al-Qaeda and ISIS/ISIL can be compared to the historical one between Marxist-Leninists and Stalinist Communists; Al-Qaeda believes in world Islamic revolution first while ISIS/ISIL believes in establishing a strong Islamic state first, and global Islamic revolution only as second priority. Just like Marxist-Leninist Leo Trotsky called for a workers' world revolution first, and Orthodox Communist Joseph Stalin in the name of a strong Communist state "socialism in one country first" put a climbing hammer through Trotsky's head instead, ISIS/ISIL are denouncing Al-Qaeda as 'sell-out infidels' while Al-Qaeda is accusing ISIS/ISIL of being barbarian terrorists (praises from Caesar). And now they are girding up to kill each other. Let's help by leaving them to it.

The second category of terrorists, are the alphabet soup of subgroups, that operate independently like franchises or are loosely 'licenced' by Al-Qaeda, including four of its official affiliates: Al-Qaeda in the Arabian Peninsula, (AQAP) in Yemen, Al-Shabaab in Somalia, Al-Qaeda in the Maghreb, (AQIM) in North Africa and the Sahel and Jabhat al-Nusra in Syria.

Within this second category are many smaller independent radical Islamist groups, including the Afghan and Pakistani Taliban, the IS group Boko Haram in Nigeria, groups in India and Bangladesh, Syria, Mali, Algeria, Jordan, Lebanon, factions in Gaza, in Malaysia and Indonesia, the Philippines, the Caucasus, western China and many other places around the world. All of them have an agenda broadly similar to that of Al-Qaeda or ISIS/ISIL to some extent.[1] Most of them are inspired and mostly funded by the Saudi Arabian radical Islamic Wahhabi cult, nicknamed "God's Terrorists" and the official state religious establishment of the Saudi Arabian Kingdom today.[2] In fact, if we wanted to really fight terrorism effectively, we should have invaded and put the Saudi Arabian state down decades ago, instead of Afghanistan and Iraq. Global

Islamic terrorism's educators and funders would have been devastated. It is no coincidence that 15 of the 19 hijackers on 9/11 were Saudi citizens.

In this book, RJ Parker looks at the third category of terrorists, the most dangerous category because they are the most unpredictable and are already living among us here in North America, perhaps even next door to you: the 'inspired terrorists', the self-radicalized Islamists who are stirred by online Islamist hate propaganda and self-trained and self-educated through online guides that instruct them on how to make improvised bombs in their Mom's kitchen and carry out mass killing attacks, increasingly without even needing to leave the borders of North America or Europe. Many of these home-grown terrorists have had previous mental health problems, criminal records and other 'misfit' behavioral issues long before they fell upon Islamic terrorism as an excuse and motive to act upon their percolating demented homicidal fantasies.

Many of these 'self-radicalized' terrorists today probably come from the same place that rampaging postal workers used to come from in the 1980s when 35 people had been killed in 11 post office shootings between 1983 and 1993.[3] Or the same place the 1999 Columbine High School massacre perpetrators Eric Harris and Dylan Klebold came from. In the world of the 2010s today, Harris and Klebold instead of being bullied 'pseudo-Goths', would have been bullied 'self-radicalized' terrorist radical Islamic coverts to ISIS—our new rising breed of mass killing zombies—impatient wannabe mass murderers who latch on to radical Islamist ideals as a license to kill a lot of people in one big suicidal blow-out.

Parker recounts in these pages some of the most notorious episodes of this home-grown Islamic terrorism that arose in the United States in recent years and threatens to only become worse.

Why do they hate us?

Although there had been warning signs in the previous decade of increasing Islamist attacks against American targets overseas, when mostly Saudi Arab Islamist terrorists destroyed the World Trade Center in New York in a Pearl Harbor-like sneak attack on 9/11, most Americans were taken by surprise and, to this day, do not quite understand why they were targeted. It was especially confounding because Americans had recently fought in the Gulf War in 1991 to free a strictly Islamic Shari's law Kuwait from a brutal occupation by the secular infidel Saddam Hussein's Iraq, a sworn enemy of radical Islamic ideology and of Al-Qaeda. bin Laden and Saddam Hussein hated each other to death.

The easiest and simplest explanation for Americans to digest and understand was the religious narrative, that somehow the 9/11 attacks were derived from a radical interpretation of Islam, that jihadi groups like Al-Qaeda and ISIS/ISIL today are driven toward an apocalyptic confrontation with Christianity in a "clash of civilizations" that political scientist Samuel P. Huntington famously warned us of as early

14

as 1993.[4]

Making matters worse, this jihadi "religious" view is also the easiest to sell to their followers by the terrorists themselves, who actually have a more complex historical perspective than solely the religious one. To understand the enemy, we need to understand the political and historical framework that underpins their hate for us. A closer examination of the history of Islamic radicalism reveals a more complex geopolitical matrix going back at least a hundred years to the nationalist Arab anti-colonial clashes with Britain and France (not the United States). The blame for the messy chaos of Iraq to Syria and Lebanon and Israel and Palestine, we can lay squarely at the feet of the British and the French, thank you very much. Britain and France, the very two countries that are now criticizing American foreign policy that is trying to clean up the mess for better or for worse, the very mess the French and British made in the first place.[5]

Then there is the perspective of internal conflicts in the Middle-East that have nothing to do with Americans or Europeans, in the form of Islamists versus their own secular governments and dictators, and the bloody internal conflict to Islam itself, between Sunni and Shiite Muslims who hate each other, a conflict comparable to the bloodbath some 400 years ago between Catholic and Protestant Christians before they learned how to live with each other.

The United States appeared to have begun meddling in these internal conflicts since 1945 and as a result made itself a target for interfering in what should have been the Middle-East's "own business." The U.S. meddling can be easily explained by its need to ensure a secure supply of oil for gas-guzzling Americans. For many Muslims, U.S. foreign policy in the Middle-East and Asia is as intrusive as if Arabs, Iranians, Pakistanis or Afghanis intervened in the issues between the Republican and Democratic Parties in the United States or in the rivalry between Christian Catholics and Protestants.

The problem at its historical core is geopolitical and not religious, but the solution might be the religious one, because in a strange way there is more that unifies Islam with Christianity and Judaism than divides us; but only if we let it.

Why They Hate Us Reason No. 1: **The Nature of the Abrahamic Religions, Jews, Christians, Muslims and "My God can beat up your God!"**

Jews, Christians and Muslims all believe that their religion descends from the same founding prophet: Abraham. Thus Judaism, Christianity and Islam are called the "Abrahamic Religions."

All three religions believe in the same god: Allah – Jehovah – God. All three religions are monotheistic in their insistence that there is only one God and his name is God. There are no other Gods permitted. Period. On that, Jews, Christians and Muslims are unanimous. Although, unlike the Jews and Muslims, the Christians do choose a fuzzy line that Jesus was a Son of God, a god himself, but also a part of a Holy Spirit Trinity that are all the same one God, in the form of three consubstantial divinities in a state of hypostases (like "compound interest or something like that" is the best I heard one priest desperately trying to explain the Trinity.)

To the monotheistic Jews and

Muslims that sounds a lot like polytheism—the pagan belief in many co-existing different gods that Imperial Roman Christianity had to comprise on in its first 400 years of growth in the Roman Empire following the execution of Jesus by Roman occupational authorities in Jerusalem somewhere between the years 33-36 AD.[6]

The Abrahamic Religions agree more or less on a whole other mess of issues. Judaism, Christianity and Islam all recognize the Old Testament Prophets, agree that Adam was the First Prophet, and all three religions revere the Biblical Prophets like Moses, Noah, Isaiah, Jeremiah, Ezekiel, etc.

Both the Muslims and the Christians recognize Christ as the Messiah – (al-Masih for Muslims), the Chosen One, whose return to the World will herald the End of Days, Armageddon, Final Judgment and Apocalypse. Both Christians and Muslims await the final return of Christ to Earth.

In Islam, Jesus is a Prophet and a Messenger of God just like Abraham and Moses, and just like Islam's final Prophet, Mohammed, the Messenger of God who came after Jesus for the Muslims. But Jesus is special for the Muslims too, as the al-Masih. However, in Islamic belief, God would never let his Prophet Jesus die cruelly in a Crucifixion. According to Islam, Allah rescued Jesus before the Romans could kill him and raised him to the heavens where he sits today near Allah, still awaiting to be returned to the World for the Apocalypse and Final Resurrection and Judgement which all the Abrahamic Religions believe in.

Christians differ in that they believe that Jesus was himself a God, a Son of God, who was born to the Virgin Mother and came in mortal form to the World, was put to death, and after three days resurrected from the dead and then ascended to the heavens where he now awaits to return to the World Resurrection and Final Judgement.

For Muslims who recognize both the Old and New Testaments, the Koran is Volume 3 completing the fundamental theology of their relationship to God.

The Jews in the meantime, reject Jesus as a Messiah and his divinity, and still await their Messiah to come. They disregard the Gospels of the New Testament and the Koran. For Jews, Jesus is a heretical Jew, which technically is exactly what he was. Indeed, Jesus was born a Jew and died a Jew. Jesus and his disciples all believed themselves as being Jews fulfilling the messianic Judaic mission on Earth. That Jesus was never a "Christian" is one of the greatest historic ironies of Christianity.

Islam as the youngest of the three Abrahamic Religions, founded in 622 A.D., because of its youth is perhaps today as recklessly strident and aggressive as its older brother Christianity was 600 years ago when it was going through its early growing pains. For what is a jihad but another word for Crusade, just like the ones the Church and the European Kings led into the Holy Lands a thousand years ago? What is the Holy Inquisition but another blood-thirsty torturing ISIS/ISIL? Islam is doing the same thing today that Christians did and that earlier before them, the Jews did, slaughter neighboring religions that do not conform to their narrow views of God. It's the nature of many religions.

Yet fundamentally we share more beliefs with Islam than conflicts, and more Muslims were murdered by other Muslims in their own sectarian conflicts than Christians were ever murdered by Muslims. And Christians have been mostly slaughtering each other (just like the Muslims) in the name of Christ long before Islam had even appeared. It was a Christian Crusader saying when approaching enemy towns with both Christian and heretic infidel populations, "Kill them all and let God sort them out." An astonishing 8 million Christians slaughtered each other in the Thirty Years War (1608-1648) between Catholics and Protestants.

So if we agree with each other on so much, why can't Christians and Muslims can't come together, except in our mutual agreement to blame all our woes on our Abrahamic elder brothers the Jews?

One reason is that Christians and Muslims, unlike the Jews, agree on one thing too many: that everybody should convert to their religion and be exactly like them. That does not leave too much room for this notion we have called "compromise" so essential to playing nice with others in a very increasingly crowded and tightly wired Planet Earth. Here we are in a Mexican stand-off unable to compromise on our two different versions of an uncompromising faith. (As for the Jews, they couldn't care less what religion anybody else is, as long as they are left alone in peace. No Jew has ever come nagging me for my conversion to their faith and way of life.)

The other reason we cannot get along is that often conflict is really never about religion in the first place, but only pretends to be. While there are many pious and good charitable mainstream religionists of all faiths, religion is often used by scoundrels as an excuse to pillage, rob, rape and conquer. To control others. To unify and enrich the rich and degrade and terrorize the poor into submission and docile servitude. Religion is often used as a flag and currency, a way of explaining long-term geopolitical issues and giving grumblers and militants some sense of identity: a brand. The Troubles in Belfast Northern Ireland, for example, were branded as "Catholic vs Protestant," and there was a certain history to conquered

Celtic Irish being associated with Catholicism and rebellion, while the conquering English were associated with the Protestant Crown and oppression. But it was not about religion; it only sounded that way.

If we look at what France and Britain did to the Arab world -- that just happened to be Islamic -- over the last 100 years, it becomes easily clear why they hate the West, that just happened to be Christian. The United States, to its credit, was a late arrival at this table of hate, but the real damage, for which the United States is paying dearly today, was done by Britain and France long before the United States arrived at the scene to contribute their own mischief in the Middle East from the 1940s onward.

Why They Hate Us Reason No. 2: The Sykes-Picot Agreement

In 1900 there was a Persian Iran but no Saudi Arabia, no Iraq, no Kuwait, no Syria, no Lebanon, no Jordan, no Yemen, no Palestine and no Israel. None of these annoyingly troubled countries existed in 1900, or even in 1915. There was only one unified Turkish Ottoman Empire, at one time an Islamic superpower that dominated the Middle-East and parts of Eastern Europe. The Ottoman Empire was also the last Islamic Caliphate (comparable to the role of the medieval Papacy in Catholicism) until it was abolished by secular modern Turks in 1924 and which ISIS/ISIL is now claiming to have re-established in Syria and Iraq.

During certain periods in its history, Ottoman Islam was tolerant of other religions and open to various currents of thought. Islamic scholars and libraries preserved Western medical, astronomical, mathematical and philosophical thought, lost in the ignorance of Dark Ages to Western scholarship. But by the 1900s, in the age of nationalism, the Ottoman Empire was beginning to come apart in

European territories like Greece, Bulgaria, the Serbian and Croatian territories; and in the Arab regions, there also was a stirring of anti-Turkish Arab nationalism. If the Greeks can have their own country broken away from the Ottoman Empire, why not the Arabs too, they asked.

Two Arab princes or Sharifs became prominent in this early stirring of Arab nationalism: Prince Abdul Aziz Ibn Saud, a tribal chief based in a tiny dusty desert oasis called Riyadh in the middle of the Ottoman Arab Peninsula, and Hussein ibn Ali al-Hashimi, the Sharif and Emir of Mecca, Islam's most holy site, located on the same Arab Peninsula but near its Western Red Sea coast in a territory at the time called Hejaz. Typically, the two Arab princes did not get along and spent more time fighting each other than freeing the Arabs from the Turks.

When in 1914 Germany and Austria went to war against the Allies—France, Britain, Russia and later the United States —in the Great War or World War I, the Ottoman Turks joined the German and Austrian side. The Turks immediately became a threat to the British and French because of their proximity to Egypt and the strategically vital Suez Canal. The fact that the Caliphate was based in Turkey, and the Emir of Mecca was under Turkish rule and could potentially bless the Turks as spearheading a jihad against infidel British and French, exposed the Allies in Egypt to a threat from their colonial troops who were Muslims at a time when the British and French could ill-afford deploying European troops to hold Egypt and the Suez.

The response of the British was twofold to this strategic threat that had potentially an Islamic jihadi undercurrent to it. Firstly, the British attempted to spark a national "jihad" of their own against the Turks, by contacting the Arabs and offering them assistance in breaking away from the Ottoman Empire. British intelligence agents, like the famous T.E. Lawrence of Arabia met with Prince Saud and Sharif Hussein (Peter O'Toole, Alec Guinness and Anthony Quinn respectively in the movie "Lawrence of Arabia") in an effort to unify the Arab tribes against the Turks with promises that after the Turks were expelled, the Arabs will join the international community as nations with Britain's and

France's backing.[7]

The British and French lied. In 1916 the French and British Foreign Ministers, Mark Sykes and François Georges-Picot, entered into a secret agreement that when the Ottoman Turks are defeated, the Arab lands and their oil reserves will be divided between themselves. The secret Sykes-Picot Agreement gave the French control of what will be artificially carved up into Lebanon and Syria, and the British what will become the artificial territories of Palestine-Israel, Jordan and Iraq. As far as the Arabian Peninsula was concerned, since nobody knew there was oil there at the time, neither the British nor French gave a damn. But just the same, not to give the other Arabs any ideas of nationhood, the British were going to renege on their promise of recognizing the territories in the Arab Peninsula as independent nations.[8]

When the war ended in 1918, and the Turks fell with the Germans and Austrians and lost their territories in the Middle-East, the British and French moved in and carved out between themselves over the 1920s and 1930s a series of artificial puppet states that became Iraq, Jordan, Syria, Lebanon,

Palestine, Yemen, Kuwait. When Saddam Hussein invaded Kuwait in 1990 claiming that Kuwait had always been a part of Iraqi territory, he was half-correct, in that neither Kuwait nor Iraq existed separately for centuries; they both had been part of the same Ottoman Empire and both were artificial creations of the British and French.

The Arabs, particularly Prince Saud in Riyadh, felt betrayed by the British and French double-dealing. This is a betrayal that the Arabs have not forgotten to this day and want undone. Anyone familiar with ISIS/ISIL political literature, knows that the "abrogation of the Sykes-Picot Agreement" is the first priority on ISIS/ISIL's non-religious political agenda.

The Rise of Radical Islam in the Middle-East: Prince Saud and the Wahhabis Cult

Just as there are many liberal versus fundamental factions and tenors of Christianity, over the years Islam too has moved to opposing poles from liberal tolerant Islam to fundamental expansionary Islam. In the 1750s, Ottoman

Islam had become confident and liberal, and some Muslim clerics began to believe it was becoming corrupt and weak in its ways, too lax and too compromising. The Ottoman Islamic establishment was accused of "losing its way," of "selling out" Islam and drifting away from the fundamental principles of Islam and the Koran.

Among the more militant and conservative of these clerics was Muhammad ibn Abd-al-Wahhab, who was so critical of establishing Islam that he was chased out by fellow Muslims from every territory in which he preached until one day in 1744. He arrived in the Saud family's oasis of Riyadh, and married a Saudi princess and found a home for his radical strictly fundamental sect of Debbie-downers that most liberal Muslims in those times loathed. And there in Riyadh the Wahhabis, as they became known, remained forever in alliance with the royal house of Saud and used Riyadh as a base for sending out Wahhabi missionaries throughout the Islamic world, preaching radical principles like women veiling themselves, a return to draconian punishments under Sharia Law, and an uncompromising hatred for other religions. In the end, the Wahhabis mostly preached and plotted against other Islamic rulers who they thought were "selling out" Islam. When the Ottoman Turks collapsed as an empire and the modern Turkish Republic became secular and abolished the Caliphate in 1924, the Wahhabi "Terrorists of God" saw this as an opportunity to make their move to dominate Islamic theology.

The Prince of Riyadh, Abdul Aziz Ibn Saud and his Wahhabi allies were not going to take the British and French betrayal of the Arabs lying down. Saud and Wahhabi warriors began waging a military campaign to seize control of the Arabian Peninsula by conquering all the neighboring territories, including those of Hejaz where the Islamic holy sites of Mecca and Medina were located under the rule of Hussein ibn Ali. Hejaz and its holy sites were conquered by the alliance of Saud and the Wahhabis in 1924-25 and Hussein was expelled and his Hashemite family was installed by the British as kings of the artificial state of Jordan, which is still ruled by the same Hussein family today.

In 1932, Prince Ibn Saud consolidated his last territory in the Peninsula and declared the founding of the Kingdom of Saudi Arabia, the Saud family's personal kingdom which the family still rules today, in a permanent alliance with the Wahhabis in Riyadh, no longer a tiny desert oasis but the capital of Saudi Arabia.

The deal struck between the Saud family and the Wahhabis was that the Saudis would control the foreign relations and economic policy of the kingdom while the Wahhabis were responsible for law, justice, religion and education. And now the Wahhabis began teaching, preaching and forcing others to practice their unforgiving and fundamental brand of intolerant and hateful Islam.

In the 1930s, an American company drilling water wells in Saudi Arabia found oil instead, and American oil companies rushed into Saudi Arabia. The first break for the American oil business in the Middle East that had been until then dominated by the French in Syria and by the British control of oil sources in Iraq, Kuwait and Persia, or Iran as it is known today. (Iranians are not Arabs, but Persians, and

Iran, although dominated by the British by the early 20th Century, had not been part of the Sykes-Picot Agreement. Persia had been an independent power for centuries, not only rivaling in the region the Ottoman Empire and Imperial Russia, but also hosting the rival minority sect of Islam, Shiite Islam, that is in opposition to the majority of Sunni Islam practiced everywhere else today. The current warring split between Sunni and Shiite Islam is as complex and as deadly as the history of conflict between Protestant and Catholic Christians in the past.)

With royalties from oil pumped by the Americans, the Saudi Kingdom now began sharing the wealth with the Wahhabi religious establishment and its militant message. When the OPEC Oil Crisis of the 1970s drove the price of oil into the stratosphere, the Wahhabis now found themselves rolling in literally billions of petro-dollars with which they began funding tens of thousands of madrassas—Islamic schools—around the world, all teaching their brand of hateful, misogynic and intolerant Islam to young impressionable boys, the future generations of jihadi warriors and terrorists around the world today. To this day, every time an American soccer mom pumps a tankful of Saudi gas in her SUV, she pays for the Saudi education and training of a young American-hating Islamic terrorist who might kill her American son or daughter one day. Today, in the Wahhabi-run school system of our "friends" the Saudis, hate of the United States and virulent anti-Semitic propaganda are part of the regular curriculum taught to Saudi youngsters.

Why They Hate Us Reason No. 3: Britain, Palestine, Israel and the U.S.

For over a thousand years, the Jews had several kingdoms of their own on the Mediterranean with their religious capital in Jerusalem. Israel and Judea were conquered by the Romans and, after a rebellion in 133–135 A.D., the Romans expelled Jews from their homeland. For nearly two-thousand years, the Jews ended up wandering stateless, often expelled from territory to territory because of Judaism's resistance to adopt the tenets of Christianity.

By 1900, what is Israel today was the province of Palestine under the rule of the Ottoman Turks. It was mostly inhabited by Muslim Palestinian Bedouin goat herders, shepherds and small farmers, who worked land owned by absentee Egyptian landowners next door. Small communities of generations of "Arabic" Jews who survived the Roman expulsions or quietly returned to the era in subsequent centuries lived in peace with their Muslim Palestinian neighbors under Ottoman Turkish rule, practicing a similar sustainable "primitive" agriculture that actually worked very well.

After World War I broke out and the British realized how vulnerable the Suez Canal could be to Turkish-inspired calls on Arab Muslims to wage a jihad against the British in the region, the British decided they needed to "buffer" the strategic Suez Canal region from the potentially expanding Islamic Arab threat next door with a non-Islamic "white" European population, and European Zionist Jews from Russia to Germany, anxious to resettle their religious homeland, fit the bill perfectly for Britain's agenda. Thus the British Balfour Declaration in 1917 which announced the British intention of finding for European Jews a national homeland "in the territory" of Palestine and to encourage Jewish migration into the region. It was not the Jewish plight that the British were concerned about; it was all about settling the territory with a people that would be friendly to British interests in the Suez Canal. Kind of like the way the British settled Protestant 'plantations' into Catholic Irish territories.

The problem was that the flood of incoming Jewish Europeans behaved in Palestine the same way French Europeans behaved in Indochina, or Spanish Europeans behaved in Central and South America, or Dutch Europeans in Indonesia, or Belgian Europeans in the Congo; they behaved like pigs toward indigenous peoples and their cultures and rights. In Palestine, arriving European Jews with their European education and modern European farming methods, and their typically racist European attitudes, saw themselves as superior to the "primitive" Palestinian goat herders and small farmers. Enterprising European Jewish settlers purchased Palestinian land from the greedy absentee Egyptian landowners, who sold out their Muslim Palestinian brothers. The European Jewish settlers began fencing off what was free range land and evicting small Palestinian farmer tenants off the land now being converted to modern European-style agricultural estates and industrial manufacturing.

By the 1940s, newly emerged neighboring countries of Syria, Lebanon, Jordan and the now almost independent Egypt, all coveted the lush territory of Palestine and its sea coast for themselves. In the hope of expelling the British from their control of Palestine and taking it for themselves, the Arab neighbors began fomenting trouble between Palestinian Arabs and Jews, often resorting to an Islamic agenda to denounce Britain's 'plantation' of non-Muslim Jews into the territory.[9]

After the Nazi Holocaust of the European Jews during the World War II, the United Nations mandated that the territory of Palestine be divided equally into two regions, one for the Palestinian Arabs and one for Jews as a homeland. The Arab League of Egypt, Syria, Lebanon, and Jordan attacked the new infant state of Israel in 1948 to seize Palestine entirely for themselves, claiming to be acting on behalf of Palestinian Arabs, who themselves were ambivalent and divided on the issue of statehood. In the end the Israelis, with U.S. aid for the first time, beat back the Arab League, and now as a victor's spoils took for themselves a huge piece of territory originally intended for the Palestinians, while the Jordanians took the other piece, known as the "West Bank" claiming they were holding it for the Palestinians. The Palestinians got nothing but were turned into a refugee nation either tolerating life under the Israelis or housed as refugees in their own land on the West Bank now claimed by the Jordanians, until the Jordanians slaughtered them all in September 1970, inspiring the name of the Palestinian terrorist group, Black September, which perpetrated the Munich Olympic Massacre. But the first Black September terrorist attacks were directed at the Jordanians, including the assassination in 1971 of Jordan's Prime Minister Wasfi al-Tal in the lobby of the Sheraton Hotel on his visit to Cairo. After shooting him, the Black September insurgent knelt and lapped up with his tongue the Jordanian Prime Minister's blood as it flowed along the hotel lobby's marble floor.

The U.S. support of Israel in the 1948 war and in subsequent wars against the Arabs in 1956, 1967 and 1973 and constant Egyptian, Syrian, Jordanian and Lebanese greed to expel the Jews and seize Palestine for themselves, expressed in terms of an Islamic jihadi struggle, began to resonate in Islamic nationalism and anti-Semitism and its association with the myth of an American-Zionist Conspiracy to conquer the Arabs and Islam. During the 1960s and 1970s Palestinian terrorist groups, or insurgents if you like, ("one man's terrorist is another man's freedom fighter") like the PLO, PDFLP, and Black September that attacked Israeli and American targets, were all secular or Marxist groups. Islam was not on their agenda; modern nationhood for a secular Palestine was. But radical Islamists in the surrounding Arab countries, hankering to take Palestine for their own, interchangeably characterize the existence of Israel as an American conspiracy or American presence in the Middle East as an instrument of a Zionist conspiracy.

As for the British and French, by then everybody had forgotten their villainy in the history of the Arab-Israeli conflicts.

Why They Hate Us Reason No. 4: U.S. Meddling in the Islamic World.

The Saudi-based Wahhabi cult during the 1920s and 1930s inspired the founding of numerous Islamic Brotherhoods in emerging secular Arab countries like Egypt, Iraq, Syria, Jordan and Lebanon. These Islamic Brotherhoods were predecessors to Al-Qaeda and were primarily engaged in terroristic acts against fellow Arab secular kings and dictators like Saddam Hussein in Iraq or Hosni Mubarak in Egypt, who in the Wahhabi tradition were seen as "selling out" Islam.

After the 1973 Arab-Israeli War and the Oil Embargo that drove OPEC oil prices sky high, radical Islamic Brotherhoods suddenly were awash in funding from Saudi Wahhabis. In 1981 an Islamic Brotherhood assassinated Egyptian President Anwar Sadat who had dared to make peace with Israel and to recognize their right to exist. In a search for stability in the Middle East, the United States, in the meantime, continued backing dictatorial secular regimes that cooperated with the U.S., which further enraged Islamic fundamentalist revolutionaries.

The Egyptian successor to Sadat, Hosni Mubarak (recently overthrown in the "Arab Spring") put the Islamic Brotherhood into cages and relentlessly pursued them to the death. Typically, although supporting Mubarak, the United States at the same time was offended by his "un-American" and less than "democratic" handling of the Islamic terrorists and eventually gave some of the accused assassins asylum in the U.S., like the Islamic Brotherhood cleric Omar Abdel-Rahman, "The Blind Sheikh" who, once safely in the United States, established a mosque in Brooklyn and gave succor to the 1993 bombing of the World Trade Center in return for the kindness and shelter given him by Americans. Today Omar is "sheltered" in a Federal Maximum Security Prison where he belongs, serving a life sentence plus fifteen years.

Iranians, in the meantime, had a long standing beef with the United States going back to 1953, when the CIA engineered the overthrow of the democratically elected moderate Iranian Prime Minister Dr. Muhammad Mosaddegh and replaced him with the tyrannical king, the Shah, Muhammad Reza Pahlavi. Known under the CIA cryptonym "Operation TP/AJAX", the clandestine action was intended to open Iran to American oil companies with whom Mosaddegh was driving a hard bargain in an attempt to get as good a deal as the Saudis had.[10] The operation, which involved spreading propaganda that Mosaddegh was communist and bribing Iranian military to cooperate in a coup, was run out of the U.S. Embassy in Tehran. Operation TP/AJAX remained secret until the 1970s when Congressional hearing revealed the hidden American hand in the overthrow of the Iranian government (along with Guatemala, Vietnam, Chile and attempts to assassinate Fidel Castro in Cuba.)

As an Islamic Shiite Fundamentalist-led revolution began to break out in Iran in 1979, the U.S. poured millions of dollars into the Shah's brutal dictatorial regime in an attempt to prop it up, triggering the Iranian revolutionaries to label the United States as "The Great Satan." When Iranian Islamic "students" overran the U.S. Embassy and took its diplomats hostage, claiming that the CIA's support of the bloody Shah regime was being run out of the U.S. Embassy compound, just like Operation TP/AJAX in 1953 was, Americans scratched their heads in a state of amnesia. (Although it should be noted, that Islamic fundamentalists in Iran in 1953 were convinced that Mosaddegh was an infidel communist and supported the CIA's overthrow of him.)

While radical Shiite Muslims now called on a jihad against the "Great Satan" U.S., the majority of radical Wahhabist Sunni Muslims who loathe the Shiites, ignored it. For a while as long as Sunnis and Shiites were too busy killing each other, we were safe from Islamist terror. When Shiite Iran went to war with secular Sunni Iraq, the United States secretly supplied weapons to Iran while it openly sold them to Iraq. All this meddling made the U.S. very few friends among the warring Sunnis and Shiites, who slowly now began to turn their attention to the U.S. as a source of their troubles.

The birth of Al-Qaeda: The Myth of American Financing

As the Soviet Union invaded Afghanistan in 1979, the Saudi Wahhabis now called for a jihad against the infidel Communist Russians. The Americans, seeing an opportunity to destabilize their Soviet Russian rivals, began to allocate weapons and funding for jihadi mujahidin (soldiers of God) to fight the Russians in Afghanistan. The U.S. did not know one mujahidin group from another, and instead of funding them directly, forwarded the weapons and money to Pakistani Inter-Services Intelligence (ISI) to distribute as they saw fit at their own discretion. The Pakistanis, who have their own ambitions in Afghanistan and who are thoroughly permeated with Wahhabi radical Islam, funded only those Afghani groups that would function as Pakistani proxies in Afghanistan once the Russians left, like the notorious Taliban which was funded by U.S. dollars filtered through the Pakistani secret services.

This is the source of the myth that Al-Qaeda and Osama bin Laden were financed and supported by the United States. They were not, because the United States did not directly fund these groups; the Pakistani ISI did. And the ISI loathed the "foreign" Saudi Arabian bin Laden and his Al-Qaeda because he was alien to Afghanistan and not controllable by the Pakistanis. The Afghanis didn't like "the Arabs" much either, as the Saudi Wahhabist radical volunteers tended to be bossy and disdainful of the "primitive" Afghani non-Arabic tribal warriors.[11] bin Laden was fortunate not to have been assassinated by the Pakistanis or the Afghani mujahidin as a meddler. bin Laden's funding came from his own family's private wealth and from Saudi Wahhabist donations to the cause from proceeds allocated by the Saudi government from oil profits.

It would be, however, the U.S.-led Desert Storm Operation against Saddam Hussein that would turn bin Laden and Al-Qaeda against the United States.

Osama bin Laden and Targeting the "Enemy Afar"

After the Russians departed Afghanistan, radical Islamic groups focused again on secular rulers in Iraq, Egypt, Syria, Jordan and other Arab countries as their enemies. Nobody paid much attention to the United States as a potential enemy. Then in 1990, Saddam Hussein invaded

Kuwait and threatened to invade Saudi Arabia. bin Laden immediately approached the Saudi Royal family and offered the services of Al-Qaeda to help expel the infidel Iraqis and defend Saudi Arabia. Instead, the Saudis invited the United States into Saudi Arabia, humiliating bin Laden and his ambitions to build a momentum for Islamic radical revolution throughout the Middle-East. When bin Laden protested, he was outlawed by the Saudis and forced to flee the country into exile. Realizing that as long as the United States was ready to protect and prop up secular dictatorial Arab regimes in their conflicts in the Middle East, there would be no hope for Islamist jihadists to take center stage, bin Laden now called on radicals to forgo targeting their nearby fellow-Arab dictators and instead target the "great enemy afar" supporting the "Zionist Conspiracy" of Israel.[12]

Starting from the humiliation of American troops in the 'holy' land in Saudi Arabia, throughout the 1990s, Al-Qaeda began increasingly focusing on American targets abroad, in the hope of suckering the United States into sending troops overseas where Al-Qaeda could get at them. While Clinton's Democratic Presidency refused to fall into the terrorists' trap, after Republican George Bush was elected to power, bin Laden saw a new opportunity to pull the U.S. into a self-destructive war in the Middle-East. On September 11, 2001, he launched the 9/11 attacks in New York City. He was hoping that the new Bush Administration would be dumber than the Clinton one. They were. Not only did the United States become stupidly mired in attempting to conventionally fight a "War on Terror" in Afghanistan, but then inexplicably proceeded to take out bin Laden's archenemy Saddam Hussein in Iraq, giving birth to the Iraqi insurgency which eventually became the ISIS-ISIL threat today.

When the Democrats returned to power in the White House under President Obama, they were no wiser than the Bush Administration, when during the "Arab Spring" they abandoned and turned their backs in the name of "democracy" on more secular regimes in the region like Egypt, Tunisia, and on Muammar Gaddafi in Libya, who was once an Islamist jihadist himself, but recently renounced his past acts of terrorism and returned to the global community of nations, albeit with a radical agenda of reparations to the Third World from former colonial powers (which is why at the behest of the Europeans, NATO chased him into a sewer pipe to die.)[13]

Thanks to British and French greed and knavery during the 1920s-1930s and some fifty years of recent U.S. policy blunders in the Middle East, the entire region is now aflame with jihadist fervor so intense that it is taking hold among American and European citizens in a form of self-radicalization, an unprecedented and dangerous new phenomenon that RJ Parker chronicles in this book.

How We Can Win the War on Terror

The overwhelming vast majority of 99.9 percent of Jews, Christians and Muslims want to raise their children in peace and prosperity and live harmoniously in respect with their neighbors. Their priority is the same as ours: the well-being of their kids, food in the fridge and a safe and secure roof over their heads, not which God their neighbor might pray to and how.

Hateful power-hungry scoundrels, whether Jews, Christians or Muslims, for centuries have been using religion as a political tool to divide and conquer people who otherwise would live and let live, by claiming that only their particular brand of religion is a "true religion" and all other beliefs are heretical and need to be rooted out by force and violence. "My God can beat up your God."

The rest of us just want to live and pray in peace in the grace and glory of our God.

The best contribution ordinary righteous Christian Americans could make to the War on Terror is to take a Muslim out for lunch and make a friend. And then invite a Jew and make another. And if any dumbass crackers object to that, all three together can put them down.

Preface

Terrorism and religious radicalization are directly proportional to each other. The spread of Islamist radicalization is what has caused the increase in terrorist activities throughout the globe. In order to curb these terrorist attacks, it is important to contain and ultimately eradicate the Islamist radicals.

Countries worldwide have increased their efforts to put a stop to terrorism, yet so far, it persists. However, in the coming ten years or so, people everywhere may see a significant decline in terrorist activities. The United States leads the offensive against terrorism, and soon it will be successful in its endeavors.

Constant strikes by Russia, United Kingdom and France, along with U.S have impacted the ISIS severely, wiping out half of their leadership, if reports are to be believed. In the coming few years, the terror group could be contained and eventually completely disbanded.

While to this day, terrorism is a massive threat that continues to loom over everybody, in the future, it might become less significant and descend into oblivion.

Radicalization

Over the years, the word 'radicalization' has taken on many different interpretations. Especially, in the last decade or so, the term radicalization has been used to define a phenomenon fast spreading in our modern world.

The word in its essence is used to describe the process through which a group or an individual starts adopting highly extremist views about a political or religious matter. It is also used in context with a situation where rebellion against the status quo erupts. Radicalization is also used to define a group of people or an individual who rejects liberal or contemporary ideas and are against freedom of speech.

In today's world, radicalization [1] has been closely associated with the ever present and persistent threat of terrorism. After the events of September 11th, 2001, the world as we knew it changed. A new order came into place; one that is very different from the bipolar or unipolar system that had prevailed. Global security became the issue at hand and countries had to come together to initiate the campaign known as 'war on terror'.

The war on terror began as a retaliation against the 9/11 attacks but quickly turned into a campaign that was fighting against an ideology, a thought process. Radicalization or radicalized individuals became the target of the military campaign that began with the United States launching an offensive against Afghanistan. The war was waged against the terrorist organization Al-Qaeda, believed to be responsible for the attacks on the World Trade Center. From then onward, the hunt began for the leaders and members of the terrorist organization who were inciting terror incidents, not just within the country but across borders as well.

Terrorism became the primary threat to global security and quickly took priority on most countries' foreign policy agenda.

This was not the first time in history that radicalization had given birth to a deadly and dangerous movement. Before the start of the Second World War, the Hitler-led Nazi campaign against the Jews was another radicalized movement that almost crippled half of the world powers. The effects of the movement were long lasting and the damage irreparable.

After the 9/11 attacks, radicalization became synonymous with the term 'Talibanization'. It is derived from the word 'Taliban' which, in essence, means student but is actually used to refer to the Afghan regime at the time of the American war. Afghanistan was under the oppressive regime of the Taliban who had established Sharia Law in the country and were promoting extremist religious views.

If you are familiar with Khalid Hosseini's work, [2] you will know that he has written a lot about the Taliban rule in the country of Afghanistan. They were a group of radicalized individuals who believed in rule by violence, terror and force in the name of religion. While the war managed to bring an end to the Taliban rule, it could not restrict the movement of Talibanization that extended after that. It began to spread across borders and led to the creation of various other terrorist factions.

Since then radicalization has been used in context to mean religious extremism or similar terrorist activities which have been the result of that.

How exactly does it occur?

It is actually a long process that takes effort and constant work. Whether the target is one individual or a group, the ultimate goal is to channel such emotions and views among them that they begin to think that violence is the only way out.

Perhaps one of the easiest and most common ways to radicalize an individual or a group is religion. No matter what, religion is one subject that can entice and provoke a person like no other. People hold their religious beliefs very dear and usually become emotionally charged when it comes to the defense of those. Hence, it is easy to manipulate or turn over a person by using their religious views against them.

Most of these terrorist groups recruit or radicalize people through different channels. They have targeted media pages which run a mass propaganda against certain entities shown as the enemy to religion, or some just rely on hate speeches and imposing their own beliefs on others. Religious extremism is centered on preaching, usually to youngsters or children bordering on adolescence and beyond. It is easier to mold a young brain than to reach out to someone who is much more aware and mature.

Over the years, radicalization has been carefully targeted and specified, especially when it comes to Islam. Islamic radicalization is believed to be the reason why the world as we know it exists. Most of the major terrorist networks have been identified as being groups of radicalized individuals who believe that they are fighting for Islam or, as it is called, 'Jihad'.

'Jihad' [3] in essence is related to defense of a religion from external or internal threats. Now these terrorists believe that it is what they are doing; the Western powers and their allies pose a threat to Islam and it is up to them to defend their religion.

Islamic radicalization has highlighted another very important aspect within world affairs. The East-West divide that has prevailed for centuries has been made even more prominent with the passage of time. Previously, ideological and cultural differences between the East and West made it difficult for the gap to be bridged. However, now there is another factor that has come into play. The threat of terrorism has led to general resentment and dissension against the Western powers within the East.

The spread of Islamic radicalization has been incremental, and now with the formation of the terror group known as ISIS, it is rearing its head as the biggest single threat to national and global security.

Islam vs the West

The East-West divide, which has further widened in the past decade or so, is the reason behind the conflict that has arisen between the two. Analysts and scholars have a number of varying opinions on the matter and have termed it as quite controversial as far as modern day politics are concerned.

Keeping the politicization of the matter aside, it can be said that the conflict between the two polarities of the world is triggered by not only ideological differences but also a power struggle. Looking at the past events of the last two decades, the conflict has only risen instead of being curbed and settled. The rise and spread of terrorism introduced the religious factor within the matter and added to the chaotic situation.

From then onward, analysts and experts started looking at the conflict as one being between Islam and the West.

Many even described it as a clash of civilizations: Islam vs the West. [4] The violent acts of terrorism that occurred in various countries throughout the world were linked to one or two very specific and extremist groups consisting of Islamist radicalized individuals.

The Islamist groups believe that they are fighting against the enemy of Islam, the West. Even the general civil population in some Islamic countries views the West as the evil oppressor who needs to be brought into submission. The resentment and dissension within the East with regard to the West was recently at an all-time high, with the Arab Spring and the ongoing Syrian conflict believed to be a result of Western interference in the Middle East.

It all started with the Iraq War in 2003, when the Bush administration invaded Iraq in an attempt to discover weapons of mass destruction being developed by the Saddam-led government in the country. This was the beginning of the Islam vs the West conflict.

Many political analysts and authors described the move as a direct intervention on the part of the Western powers within the East. Not just the Middle Eastern countries became wary; the feeling of resentment among the general public also rose. This clash of civilizations is what prompted these radicalized Islamists to spread their operations in an effort to retaliate against the Western powers.

The conflict also highlights the long standing hostility between the Muslim countries and the state of Israel. Most of the Muslim states have opposed Israel's influence in the West and expressed dissatisfaction over the Western powers' role in the Palestine-Israel conflict. The combination of all these factors have made it quite difficult for both the western and eastern sides to curb the animosity that is strengthening with time.

There are a number of reasons which have caused the divide between the two sides to grow further and further. The inherent difference lies in the sociological, ideological and cultural values found on both sides of the world. Experts believe that the foundation of the divide was laid out centuries ago when the clash between Christianity and Islam occurred.

In the modern times, the conflict between the two sides became more of a clash of ideologies. Many different scholars have much to say and write about this. A number of them believe that the conflict arises as a result of the different social and cultural norms present on either side. The West believes in equal rights, gender equality, freedom of speech and a democratic system, while the East is much more orthodox and restrictive with their system of government and societal norms.

With the spread of Islamic radicalization, these differences have become even more prominent. The Islamists are looking to impose Sharia Law within their territories; their views are extremist and there is no freedom of anything. The terrorist networks that carry out these activities claim that the reason behind these acts of terror is Islam. They want to stop the Western influence and put an end to the freedom of speech, gender equality and take away the rights of women.

Whether it is the Al-Qaeda, the Taliban or the recently formed ISIS, all of them raise the slogan of Islam and claim that their fight or 'Jihad' is against the

Western influence. If you are one to closely follow global affairs, then you must be well aware of the activities of the ISIS, now known as the Islamic State (IS). They are a group of highly radicalized individuals who have carried out beheadings, bombings and mass murder, all in the name of Islam.

The Islam vs the West debate can be better understood with reference to some Middle Eastern and South Asian countries. The particular countries have been the ones affected the most in the conflict that arose when the West exerted its influence within the East in an attempt to bridge the gap between the two sides. After the Iraq war, tensions were running high, and the Eastern countries were making drastic changes to their foreign policies with regard to the West. The Western powers, led by the United States of America, were trying to stabilize the situation but to no avail.

When the Obama administration came in, the ties between the West and the East slightly recovered and looked to be on the mend. However, before significant progress could take place, the Arab Spring originated in 2011 and the turmoil in the East peaked within a short span of time.

The Arab Spring was a wave of revolution that started out in Tunisia and soon engulfed most of the Middle Eastern countries as well as a few North African ones. Civil uprisings and revolutions started out in Egypt, Libya, and Yemen, going all the way to Algeria, Iraq, Morocco, Oman, and Sudan, with a few minor protests being demonstrated in Saudi Arabia as well. As a result of these civil movements, many regimes and rulers had to fall back, with temporary governments being put in place of them. The movement went on for a year and a half as the pro-government forces did their best to subdue the civil unrest.

In some countries, the counter demonstration and pro-government forces fought the protesters off with violence while in others the protesters were able to fend some off. There are other countries like Syria, where the unrest culminated in a full-blown civil war that is ongoing to date. Perhaps, the most profound effect that movement had was on the countries of Syria and Libya. Both of these countries saw extreme violence and a high amount of casualties when civil war broke out.

The Western involvement in this movement has raised quite a few questions as far as the aftermath is concerned. Scholars have debated whether the involvement of the West has actually given rise to the turmoil or helped in bringing an end to it. Political analysts believe that the distrust within the East against the West has only increased during this time, particularly with regard to the West's role in the Syrian War.

Another important aspect within the Islam vs the West debate is the role of certain Islamic countries with regard to the Western influence. The United States of America is integral within South Asia, especially when it comes to the countries of India and Pakistan. Both these countries have been side by side with America in the war against terror and, as a result, have had to bear the brunt of retaliation by the terror groups. The impact on Pakistan, in particular, has to be highlighted here, due to its role in the war against terror. The country borders with Afghanistan and has been known to provide refuge to the highest number of migrants that made the cross border journey after war broke out in their country.

The reason why Pakistan is of importance in this debate is because of the events that followed afterwards. The country was hit by a wave of terrorist bombings, mass murder and political assassinations claimed to be carried out by extremist Islamist groups. A number of terrorist factions sprang up, with many of them being under the influence of Taliban leaders. The governance reached out to the West for help when terrorism within the country began to peak.

A mountainous area high up in the country, known as North Waziristan and believed to be the hub of all terrorist activities, saw a military action taken up by the Pakistan army along with the help of the United States. American drones attacked many terrorist hideouts and managed to take out terrorist leaders of note.

The role of the West in the region has not been viewed favorably. Many see it as another attempt made by the Western powers to intervene in the internal affairs of the country and pose a threat to its sovereignty. This has only added to the conflict between the two polarities of the East and West. The West and Islam once again face off against each other, with the former being posed as a threat to the latter.

The general opinion within the region is that the West is exerting its power and influence to wipe out Islamic values and their cultural norms. Hence, the opposition that the Western powers face is not only from the terrorist organizations, but also from the civilians suffering from the instability and turmoil in the region.

During this time, the West also had to deal with another stagnant problem, which is presented by the terror group IS. The militant group has been known to expand their operations and has claimed responsibility for a number of terrorist attacks on Western soil.

All of these factors have only emphasized the divide that culminates in the Islam vs the West conflict. While the social and ideological differences had always been there, the ties between the East and the West were seemingly not as bad as they appear to be in the past few years.

Actually, it is not about the East and West now; instead Islamic radicalism has made it about religion vs the West. These Islamists strongly believe that they are defending their religion of Islam. What is interesting to note here is that Islam, in its essence, has nothing to do with terror.

A Failed Ideology

The debate between the West and Islam draws a lot of focus on the ideological differences [5] that underline the problem. The basis of the divide between the West and East is ideology. While the Western ideology promotes liberalism and freedom, the Eastern ideology is more conservative and orthodox.

In recent times, the ideological conflict between the two sides has been further highlighted by the rapid spread of Islamism. The Islamists are a minority of people who believe that Islamic countries should be run on the fundamental model of Islam presented by the Prophet Muhammad in Medina. Muhammad, the last messenger of God, is a role model for Muslims across the world.

The Islamists believe in the fundamentals of Islam very strongly and are of the opinion that a similar caliphate should be established in the Muslim world.

Radicalized Islamists are those who have actually taken it upon themselves to ensure that such a model is implemented. An example of such a case is the terrorist group, Islamic State (IS), whose leader has proclaimed himself as the Caliph leader of all Muslims.

A clash of ideologies between the two sides is not new. It has prevailed since a long time past; however, in the past few decades or so, it has culminated in a conflict that has impacted both sides negatively. While the West tries to bridge these gaps and strengthen ties in the region, the constant turmoil and instability holds the East back from reciprocating.

The rise of terrorism has caused further dissension and chaos, with the political and economic situation in the region deteriorating rapidly. Furthermore, the ongoing Syrian conflict has only added to the tension. On the forefront of this ideological clash is Iraq, which was invaded by the United States in 2003. It was this war which gave rise to the radicalized Islamists, with Iraq providing the breeding space for these Islamists and their ideologies to thrive.

The Western-led war on terror after the 9/11 incident was a campaign to counter terrorism and take out terrorist groups. It soon became a war against an ideology, an extremist school of thought.

It has been argued that the West has tried to take advantage of their war against terror campaign and used it to assert its power and influence in the region. Many critics of the Western policies have stated that the turmoil and instability in the region is actually a result of the interventionist policy pursued by the Western states. These critics believe that the West tried to impose its own ideology within the region, and that backfired when the situation only deteriorated further instead of improving.

The incremental increase in terror groups and activities was in retaliation against this Western ideology that was being imposed. Analysts believe that the radicalized Islamists rose to counter the Western ideology and curb its influence.

Whatever the case, the Islamist ideology has failed to achieve its aim so far. Islamic radicalization is restricted to a minority of people; however, its influence has spread far and wide. It has given birth to different terrorist factions and groups situated in various locations across countries and borders. These groups and factions in turn are responsible for most of the terrorist activities that wreak havoc upon innocent civilians and give rise to instability.

Terrorism is one of the primary threats to global security, and that is why the West has also increased their efforts to counter it. Apart from the drone attacks in North Waziristan, there has also been a military offensive launched against the Islamic State that claimed responsibility of the Charlie Hebdo attacks as well as those in Paris.

The ideological clash between the East and the West has contributed significantly to the rise of these Islamic fundamentalists. The economic, social and political divide between these two polarities has only widened with time, and little can be said about the future. Tensions heightened during the Arab Spring movement, and resentment against Western policies began to increase.

Western powers were of the opinion that the situation could be controlled with the right directive, but it only worsened.

What the Western powers did not realize at the time was, that the region was not ready for an ideological change. Years of colonialism, imperialism and an ever-increasing North-South gap has led to distrust and dissension among the people as far as the Western policies are concerned. This is what spurs the clash of civilizations that many noted scholars have talked about.

This clash of civilizations has now been narrowed down to a conflict between the West and Islamization. The Western powers oppose the Islamization that promotes radicalism and extremism and stands against everything the West believes in. It can be said that the ideology behind Islamization has failed up until now and has done little to counter Western influence.

So why has this ideology failed?

The answer is simple. It has only managed to exert whatever little influence it could through terrorism and radicalization. The Islamist ideology works on extremist views and forceful imposition, hence, it fails to attain its objectives.

As mentioned before, author Khalid Hosseini has written a lot about the rule of the Taliban in Afghanistan before the American war. The Taliban ruled the country under Islamization, and his books have a detailed and thorough description of what life was like for the average citizen under that regime. When the Americans launched their military offensive against Afghanistan, the rule of the Taliban fell and, in a sense, Afghanistan was actually liberated.

While the oppressive regime was over, the thought and ideology was still prevalent and, over the passage of time, has managed to spread farther as well. The spillover effects were felt across borders when the terrorist activities not only increased within the region but also in the neighboring countries.

More recently, the Islamist ideology is represented by the Islamic State. The group, whose rise can be charted back to a couple of years, has been responsible for a number of terrorist activities not just in the Eastern region but also some of the Western countries. As of now, efforts are being made to eradicate the influence of the militant group and break down their network.

Islamic Terrorism

Charting the Course

Islam and terrorism have become synonymous with each other. While the threat of terrorism has taken center stage only after the September 11 attacks, it was present since a long time before. Islamic terrorism is a phenomenon that has emerged recently and is spreading fast throughout the world.

Basically, Islamic terrorism comprises those terrorist activities that are conducted in the name of Islam. These acts of terror are carried out on a global scale, both in the non-Muslim and Muslim countries. In fact, the countries that are most affected by terrorism are majorly the Muslim majority states in South Asia and North Africa.

While the rise of Islamic terrorism is fairly recent, the history behind its evolution goes decades back. Modern Islamic terrorism started in the 1960s when

Palestinian Liberation movements [6] and freedom fighters shifted from the old methods of guerrilla warfare to urban terrorism. They felt that these terrorist acts would be far more effective in the achievement of their objectives rather than their previous methods. Radical Palestinians, with the help of communication and the transportation system, turned their struggle around. A series of kidnappings, political assassinations, bombings and murders were carried out which soon branched out internationally.

The Palestinian network worked as a successful model for other terrorist entities that started learning their techniques and tactics in order to further their own movements. The rise of nationalism in the Arab states and radical Islamic movements brought about the formation of these groups that aimed to achieve their objectives and oppose secularism through terrorism. Conservative Arab regimes were not open to political Islam and progressive change; hence, they supported anti-nationalist groups that were against secularism and political Islam.

The era following that was the real turning point in the case of Islamic terrorism. In 1979, the Iranian revolution sparked fear against the spread of Shiite Islam. Apart from that, the Soviet Union invasion of Afghanistan in the same year also contributed to the advent of Islamic terrorism groups. The invasion is actually believed to be the reason why the terrorist groups of Al-Qaeda and factions of the Taliban came into existence. The mujahideen consisting of radical Afghans who fought against the Soviet forces are believed to be responsible for the formation of these groups.

At the time, these terrorist factions were state sponsored and backed by different countries pursuing their own individual agendas. When the Soviet forces withdrew, only then did the consequences began to present themselves. In the 1990s, the Taliban movement started out in Afghanistan and ultimately came into power.

Insurgency related violence and terrorism on an international level began to rise in a number of the Middle Eastern states. Yemen, Libya and Lebanon saw an exponential increase in terrorist groups and activities. These groups have been active on a number of fronts, both domestic and international. Hezbollah, a Lebanon-based radical Shiite group formed in the early 1980s, has been involved in the training and arming of both Shiite and Sunni movements.

All these terrorist groups harbor a strong anti-west sentiment and have been known to carry out terrorist attacks on Western soil.

The culmination of Islamic terrorism was the 9/11 incident. It not only shook the world's most powerful nation but also brought about a new world order. Since then Islamic terrorism has become a matter of global security. The Western powers came together to thwart such terrorist activities and put an end to these movements. However, there has been little success up until now on that front.

Instead of receding, these terrorist groups have further branched out and advanced their networks. Many of them even have global bases across Europe, North and South America, Africa and Asia.

The activities have also become more destructive and violent. Mass bombings and shootings are carried out commonly in North Africa, South Asia and some Middle Eastern regions as well. More recently, the Western countries have been targeted as well.

When the United States invaded Afghanistan in 2001, they managed to bring an end to the Taliban regime. However, the Islamist ideology still prevailed. The spillover effect of that was felt in the neighboring regions, especially the territory of Pakistan. The country had hosted millions of Afghan refugees fleeing from the war, and that gave rise to a number of problems within.

Different terrorist factions began to emerge, establishing bases in the northern areas of the country, especially the region bordering with Afghanistan, North Waziristan, became the hub of all terrorist activities. Large scale terrorist attacks both in the urban cities and rural areas became frequent and the country had to launch an internal military initiative to gain control of the situation. In the North Waziristan region, the United States, Pakistan's major ally in the war against terror, conducted drone attacks targeting terrorist hubs and hideouts.

In an interesting turn of events, the hunted Al-Qaeda leader, Osama bin Laden, mastermind of the 9/11 attack, was discovered within Pakistan territory in a city called Abbottabad. The United States Secret Service and Intelligence carried out an on-ground military operation and were able to successfully take down the leader of the militant organization.

As far as international Islamic terrorism is concerned, it is still as prevalent as it was a few years ago. While the efforts made by the Western states and their allies have managed to curb it to some extent, the threat is still very much present. Now, more than ever, the threat posed by Islamic terrorism seems to be looming everywhere. The Islamic State, IS, a deadly terrorist organization, based out of Iraq and known for their heinous acts of beheading, rape and mass murder, is becoming more influential by the day. They have claimed responsibility for various terrorist attacks across Europe and North America.

Islamic terrorism has caused destruction and damage on a wide scale. In countries of North Africa and South Asia, it also contributes to political instability and economic recession. As a result of these terrorist activities, economic progress slows and foreign investment almost becomes negligible, which not only destabilizes the government but also results in civil unrest. For example, in a country that is dependent on foreign aid and investment for economic progress, terrorism is a setback.

Islamic terrorist movements have been primarily targeting the developing countries. The impact on them is much stronger as they are still politically and economically weak. This is exactly why countries like Afghanistan, Iraq and a few others have become the breeding ground for such terrorist groups.

Up until a few years ago, these terrorist groups restricted their activities to Middle Eastern, South Asian and African states. However, their recent targets were major Western states across the European and North American regions. In Paris, France, mass shootings and suicide bombings [7] claimed the lives of almost a hundred and thirty people. These coordinated attacks were carried out by Islamist terrorists, believed to be involved with the Islamic State.

Just a year before, another terrorist incident which made headlines was an attack on an Army school in the city of Peshawar, Pakistan. [8] A radical group was behind the mass shooting that claimed the lives of more than one hundred and forty people, most of them students under the age of thirteen.

Over the past few years, an increase in such coordinated terror attacks has led to military offensive being launched against these Islamic terrorist groups. The United States, Russia, United Kingdom and France have carried out air strikes in areas where these terrorist groups have established bases. The Islamic State, for example, is based out of Northern Iraq and Syria, and have had a number of their bases destroyed by missiles in these air strikes. Especially after the Paris attacks, the military offensive became even more aggressive than before, with France and Russia both carrying out frequent air strikes within territories known to be harboring the

Islamic States militants.

Looking back, it can be said that while the spread of Islamic terrorism is recent, the thought behind it has been there a long time. Previous acts of terrorism carried out by Islamists were not as wide scale and coordinated as they are now. Extremists from Chechnya, Libya, Lebanon and a number of other Middle Eastern states were trained and armed in camps situated across European, American and African countries.

This movement actually spread during the 1980s when mass radicalization among concentrated groups occurred. It gained momentum during the late 1990s and culminated due to the events of 9/11, after which the world powers combined to act against it.

From 2001 onward, Islamic terrorism has been a threat to global security, political stability and economic reform. Particularly in the developing world, acts of terrorism can cause a major economic setback and result in extensive long-term damage. If one is to take the example of Afghanistan, one can see how terrorism has impacted the economic and political stability within the country. Their survival is purely dependent on foreign aid which has prevented it from descending into oblivion.

Some of the South Asian countries like Pakistan, Bangladesh and even India have been affected by this rapid spread of Islamic terrorism. Terrorist attacks in the region have claimed the lives of thousands and remain a threat to political regimes within these countries.

In the last few years, despite the constant efforts of the world powers, the threat of terrorism has become more prominent and stronger than ever before. Islamic State, or ISIS as it is referred to, raised its flag in northern Iraq, establishing a base in the city of Mosul. This group claimed that it wanted the Islamic world to be modeled as a Caliphate, just as it was in the time of the Prophet Muhammad. The leader of the group was proclaimed the Caliph with the members of the group swearing allegiance to him. Not only that, a number of various other terrorist groups also came under their banner and now identify themselves as an extension of the

Islamic State.

Boko Haram, [9] an extremist group based in Nigeria and operating in most of the North African countries, came under the IS banner. All of their terrorist activities are now carried out in the name of the terrorist organization. Like the IS, they also believe that their acts are a part of 'Jihad' , which in Islam is described as fighting for the religion against enemy propaganda. It came into global media's attention in 2014, when 276 girl students were kidnapped from an area in the country called Chibok. [10]

The leader of the group announced that they were behind the kidnapping of the girls and it had been done with the intention of selling them as slaves. This incident created quite a stir internationally, with campaigns being run on the social media in order to bring it to the world leaders' attention. Celebrities, politicians and business leaders asked for a combined effort to be made for the release of the students.

In Nigeria itself, the criticism against the government and political leaders saw posters being hung on the street carrying the slogan 'Bring back our girls'. Other than that, the terrorist group has been known to carry out frequent bombings, massacres and shootings in an attempt to destabilize the government and the region.

Its operations spread out to the Cameroon, Chad and other North African regions where it has claimed responsibility for several acts of terror. The government and political leaders have sanctioned military actions against the group and, according to recent claims, the military has been successful in eradicating their influence within the region to a great extent.

Islamic State gained the attention of the world during 2014, when their brutal acts of terror were broadcast on social media and on television channels as well. They started out by establishing control over territory in Iraq and soon went on to war-ridden Syria. Since then the group has been involved in various terrorist activities both within their region and outside.

Human rights violations, maltreatment of civilians and mass beheadings have been some of the acts of utter brutality that have made headlines throughout the world. On October 31, 2015, a Russian plane crash which ISIS claimed responsibility for, [11] as well as bombings in Beirut, attacks in Paris and a few political assassinations. All of this led to a combined military and strategic counter defense involving a number of countries being carried out against the terrorist organization.

Critics of the ideology behind Islamic terrorism argue that all activities carried out in the name of Islam are not only non-Islamic but anti-Islam. Journalists and scholars have written about this extensively, expressing their views about the matter. Some are of the opinion that Islam and Sharia Law [12] might actually be the catalyst that have prompted these acts of terror and given rise to terrorism. There are others whose opinion differ from that; they argue that these terrorists are just behind religion and using it as a platform or a facade to further their own individual agendas. Examples from Islamic verses and quotations have been cited to support their view that Islam does not support or promote terrorism.

Like every argument, there are two sides to this as well. Nothing can be stated for certain. Critics of Islam have identified several incidents from Islamic history and verses from the holy book of Muslims, the Koran, which support their view that the religion incites violence and established dominance by force. This has led to the generation of a number of conspiracy theories regarding the spread and rise of Islamic terrorism.

According to polls and surveys conducted by several news channels, the general Muslim view is that these Islamic terrorists distort Islam and their cause is in no way related to religion. The youth, especially, is of the opinion that just a small minority of people are under the influence of this radicalization and the majority of them stand against it.

NEXT **At Home in America**

The Boston Marathon Bombings

The Boston Marathon bombings created a furor throughout the world with countries of the world expressing solidarity and a strong resolve to end the plague that is terrorism. The problem that had been persistent in the developing world now seemed to be spreading over to the more developed countries across the globe.

April 15, 2013, initially began as any other normal day in the city of Boston, Massachusetts, with the exception of the annual Boston Marathon [13]. At the finish line, things took a turn for the worse when two bombs targeted the runners and spectators, killing three and wounding over 260 people. There were two terrorists believed to be involved in the attacks, and they were hunted down within days. According to reports, the terrorists were not members of any terrorist organization and had been acting individually. One of the terrorists caught was sentenced to

death in June 2015.
***

    The Boston Marathon is one of the oldest events held in the city and marks the annual Patriot's Day in Massachusetts. Patriot's Day is recognized as a day that commemorates the battles which started the historic American Revolutionary War. The marathon is actually a historic event significant throughout the globe as an annual event held in honor of the 1775 battles of Lexington and Concord. It is a legal holiday throughout Massachusetts on the third Monday of April.

    On the day of 117th Boston Marathon, the races began without any sign of an imminent attack. The spectator areas along the route had been checked for bombs and other deadly devices twice. There was a gap of one hour between the last bomb sweep and the setting off of the bombs. Spectators and other people had been freely coming in and going out in that time with unchecked bags and items surrounding the race area.

    The atmosphere in the city is usually festive as thousands of observers turn out to watch the athletes that take part in the marathon. These spectators surround the more than twenty-six-mile-long route, starting from Hopkinton, Massachusetts, and going all the way to the Back Bay neighborhood, which is located in Boston.

On April 15, 2013, the marathon started with almost twenty-three-thousand participants running, jogging, and some just walking the marathon merely to take part. At 9:32 a.m., the race officially began as the elite women runners set off. They were soon followed by the top male runners along with hundreds of others coming in as the first wave passed by at 10:00 a.m. There were additional waves of runners who started the race between 10:20 and 10:40 a.m.

The first person to cross the finish line was Kenyan athlete Rita Jeptoo; she made it across the 26.2-mile route in two hours, fifty-six minutes and twenty-five seconds. The men's winner, Lelisa Desisa from Ethiopia, made it through the finish line in two hours, ten minutes and twenty-two seconds. Both winners ran through eight of the Bay State towns and cities to reach the finish line.

At 2:49 p.m., roughly two hours after the winners had crossed the finish line and five hours into the race, the first bomb exploded. About six thousand runners were yet to finish, and the bomb went off amongst the spectators standing around the finish line. It detonated about half a block away from the finish line, on the north side of Boylston Street, near Copley Square.

Just twelve seconds later, another bomb went off around the same area, about 180 to 190 metres apart from the first. The investigation later showed that these two bombs were known as 'pressure cooker bombs' [14] and were packed in with shrapnel along with other deadly substance. According to initial reports, these bombs had been hidden in a backpack which had been placed near the finish line in the spectator area.

The first bomb that went off was placed outside the Marathon Sports which is at 671-673 Boylston Street. Investigators recorded the exact time of the explosion as 2:49:43 p.m. Now during the time of the explosion, the clock at the finish line was displaying the time at 4:09:43 and this reflected the time elapsed since the last wave of the runners had started off at 10:40 a.m. The second explosion occurred about twelve seconds after the first with the recorded time being 2:49:57 p.m. It was not even at a far distance from the first one, just a block away, farther west, around 755 Boylston Street.

Both of those bomb explosions were sudden and had a strong impact on the buildings along the street as well. While structural damage had been avoided, the windows of the adjacent buildings were blown out. Even after the explosions went off, before the police were able to secure the area off completely, many athletes and runners continued to pass through the finish line. Reports state that approximately eight minutes after the blasts were heard, participants were crossing the finish line.

Those blasts caused the otherwise peaceful and fun-filled festivities to descend into complete chaos. The scene which was being enjoyed by spectators, who had come to support the athletes and commemorate the historic day, had turned into a site of death and destruction. The explosions claimed the lives of three innocent civilians and left around two hundred and sixty-four wounded.

The dead civilians were spectators who had been standing around the finish line near the area where the bombs had been placed. When they went off, these three people were the first victims. [15]

Krystle Campbell, 29

Martin Richard, 8

Lu Lingzi, 23

Among the injured, there were quite a few who were in grave danger. Sixteen of those gravely wounded victims ended up losing their legs, with the youngest one to suffer amputation being a seven-year-old girl.

***

In the immediate aftermath of the bombings, first responders [16] rushed to the destruction and injured people. The medical tent that had been set up to help and treat the athletes who were running, was turned into a medical emergency camp within minutes. The three civilians were declared dead while a hundred of the wounded victims were transferred to local area hospitals. City police and federal investigators present on the scene closed the area off as the crime scene was surveyed around fifteen square blocks.

Other rescue workers, bystanders and media personnel who were close by also got to the crime scene immediately and started helping the emergency first responders treat the injured. Additional teams and units from the Boston Fire Department, Boston Emergency Medical Services and Boston Police Department were dispatched to assist. Along with that, request for mutual aid was put forward and a number of private ambulances responded to it.

The explosions which had claimed the lives of three and injured hundreds more led to the city being closed off for an indefinite time. Emergency alerts were sent out to hospitals as twenty-seven of those got ready to receive the gravely wounded victims. Most of the victims that were admitted to these twenty-seven local hospitals were bystanders who had been standing around the blast site. Fourteen people had to undergo immediate amputation surgeries, with some even going through traumatic amputations as a result of being under direct impact of the blasts.

Races were halted and the Marathon was brought to an abrupt stop. The Boston Police followed emergency protocol and started diverting the remaining runners still on course to the finish line, away from it. Runners were told to take an alternate route going towards Boston Common and the Kenmore Square. The buildings nearby, along with Lenox Hotel, were evacuated and eventually closed off for the day.

The Police also sealed the fifteen-block area around the blast site. On April 16th, this was reduced to a twelve-block crime scene narrowed down by the investigators and police officers.

The Massachusetts Army National Guard soldiers who were present on the scene started helping the local teams and authorities in providing aid to the injured. The Boston Police Commissioner immediately issued a statement advising people to stay in and off the streets for the rest of the day. In the chaos that ensued after the explosions went off, the civilians who were fleeing the scene dropped off their backpacks and other items that were all looked upon as potential threats after the police took control of the site.

A panic search that was carried out to survey these potential threats led to a number of conflicting reports being sent out. It was initially stated that more explosive devices and bombs had been discovered around the area, after which there were reports of the Boston Police Bomb Squad intending to carry out a controlled explosion around the 600 block on Boylston Street. However, in the end, no such bombs or explosive devices were discovered, and all of these reports were rendered as misguided.

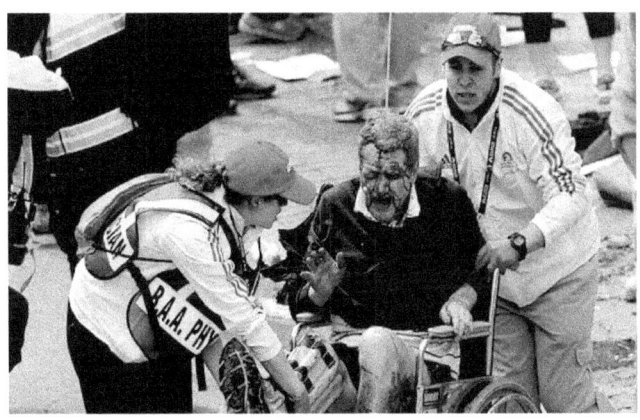

One man had both legs blown off

Carlos Arrdondo of Costa Rica helps the same man in previous picture. Once strangers, they remain friends today.

The body of Krystle Campbell, 29, in blue shirt at the bottom of this picture

Some media outlets also started reporting about an alleged bombing incident at the John F. Kennedy Presidential Library which is situated within the Dorchester section of the city. This led to the Navy sending out its bomb disposal unit to the City of Boston in order to assist the local police and authorities with these situations. It turned out that the reports of the bombing at the library were untrue and it was just an unrelated fire that started as a result of an electrical problem.

As a precautionary measure, the Federal Aviation Administration ordered the airspace above Boston as a restricted fly zone and even issued a ground stop effective immediately at Boston's Logan International Airport. Some of the services of the Massachusetts Bay Transportation Authority were also halted. Many other cities in the state of Massachusetts, as well as other nearby states, were put on alert with police forces and hospital staff being on emergency standby.

The United States Attorney General issued a statement directing that the United States Department of Justice lay down their 'full resources' and do everything they can to investigate the explosions.

The City of Boston had been shaken by these explosions. There was panic and chaos as people tried to reach out to their family and friends in the vicinity. The police and authorities were doing everything they could to assist everyone in need of help.

The Massachusetts Emergency Management Agency sent out a message to the people who were trying to contact their family and friends in the city, saying that those who were unable to reach their loved ones should try using text messages instead of voice calls. The cellphone lines were crowded due to the flood of calls that came pouring in as the news of the bombings made headlines across the globe. Despite being congested, the cellphone service in Boston remained in operation, even after some rumors began circulating that the cellphone service was being shut down to prevent the phones from being used by criminals as detonators.

The American Red Cross unit helped by assisting the concerned people in obtaining information regarding their friends, families and the runners in the marathon. People were put in touch with respective hospitals so that they could be informed and updated regarding the casualties. The Boston Police Department was also able to set up a running helpline, making it relatively easier for the people to contact friends and family in the area. There was another line which was separately set up to provide people with information regarding the victims and wounded.

Google activated their Person Finder, which is a disaster service that helps locate people. The Google Person Finder listed a log of all the missing persons under 'Boston Marathon Explosions' with known information. People were able to view this log publicly and find information on their person of concern.

The people of Boston rose to the emergency occasion magnificently. They came to the aid of the injured, helped with transportation, and those who were stranded on the streets due to the area being closed off. The nearby hotels and buildings around the blast site had been evacuated and sealed off; this left a number of people out on the streets with nowhere to go. A number of the local residents opened their own homes to these people and gave them a place to stay.

***

Just in a day, a wide-scale investigation involving a thousand officers belonging to federal agencies, state and local departments, as well as other law enforcement agencies in the city was launched. It continued on for two days until a breakthrough occurred when analysts belonging to the Federal Bureau of Investigation were able to pinpoint a couple of suspects.

The FBI, leading the investigation, was assisted by a number of other agencies; the Bureau of Alcohol, Tobacco, Firearms and Explosives, the National Counter-terrorism Center, the Central Intelligence Agency, and the Drug Enforcement Agency, were all part of the investigation that was being conducted throughout the city in a search for the bombers.

FBI analysts went through thousands of pictures and footage from security and closed-circuit cameras around the blast site before they were able to identify two primary suspects. United States government representatives and officials issued a statement saying that these bombings had been a sudden act of terror as they had no prior intelligence reports which indicated that such an incident could take place. Representative Peter King, who was also a member of the House Intelligence Committee, said that he had been briefed during two top-secret meetings regarding potential terror threats within the United States, and there was no report which could have been possibly tied to the occurrence of this unfortunate event.

When the possible suspects had been pinpointed, the FBI released images of the two men, which had been picked up by surveillance cameras. Following that, they were soon able to identify the possible suspects. The father of these two men later came forward, saying that the FBI had been keeping a close watch on his family and had even questioned the men before in Cambridge, Massachusetts. According to his claim, the family had been subjected to questioning five times regarding possible explosions within the streets of Boston and in relation to terrorist groups.

During the investigation, the officials at the site found shrapnel which included parts of various metals, ball bearings, and nails as well as pieces of black nylon. The nylon pieces were later found to be blown off from a backpack. There was also a pressure cooker lid that was discovered on the rooftop of a nearby building. The investigating officials also found the remains of an electric circuit board and wires which had been scattered during the blast.

All the evidence collected from the blast site was sent to the laboratory at the Federal Bureau of Investigation for a detailed analysis. It was later revealed that those bombs were improvised explosive devices (IED) known as pressure cooker bombs and manufactured by the bombers themselves. The authorities also reported that the bombers had found the instructions to manufacture these bombs in a magazine allegedly published by Al-Qaeda and circulated within the Arabian Peninsula.

When the suspects had been identified, The Boston Globe newspaper published a report on the investigation in

114

which it stated that one of the suspected bombers had bought fireworks from a fireworks store located in New Hampshire. A few days after the suspected bombers were revealed, the FBI, along with the West New York Police Department and Hudson County's Sheriff Department, located the suspect's sister and found incriminating evidence in her apartment. The officials seized all the computer equipment from the apartment that was situated in West New York, New Jersey.

A week later, the FBI and the Department of Homeland Security issued a joint intelligence bulletin [17] disclosing the details of the investigation. According to a report, the bulletin included the preliminary analysis of every recovered device brought in from the site of the crime. The report also stated that the investigators had even found evidence leading to the detonation of the bombs. They believed that the two bombs which had been manufactured at home, were triggered through long-range remote control devices that are usually used to operate toy cars. The investigators also finished a preliminary reconstruction of the pressure cooker bombs that had been used in the Boston Marathon attacks.

***

A news conference was held on April 15, two days after the Boston Marathon attacks, during which the FBI officials released the surveillance footage and photographs of the two suspects they believed were the bombers. The conference was described by the authorities as being the 'turning point' in the investigation.

Public help was sought in order to identify these suspects, who were shown in photographs and video, carrying backpacks and walking in a single-file formation. The two men were picked up by the cameras walking nonchalantly but purposefully. A security camera around the area caught one of the suspects surveying the site just minutes before the blast; his Bridgestone hat stood out in the surveillance video that had been released.

The FBI is thought to have released some of these photos, in part, to control the damage which had been done by the false news reports and rumors that had been generated by news media and television channels. These photos could help those who had been wrongly targeted on social media or by incorrect news reports.

Investigators and officials received a lot of assistance and co-operation on part of the victims as well as the bystanders that led them to the suspects. Jeff Bauman, one of the gravely injured victims who ended up losing both his legs after coming under direct impact of the explosions, had been standing adjacent to the location of one of the bombs. When Bauman regained consciousness in the hospital, he asked for a pen and paper to write something. After being provided those, he wrote a note to the FBI investigators that said, '*bag, saw the guy, he looked right at me*'. Bauman later recovered enough to provide a detailed description to the FBI and other authorities of the suspect who had been seen placing a backpack right beside him. The bomber had placed this backpack at the blast site just two-and-a-half minutes before it went off.

Mr. Bauman's description and details about the incident helped the investigators greatly. The suspected perpetrator in the photo was identified quickly and his picture was circulated within media channels.

According to the investigating officials, the yet unnamed suspects were initially referred to as 1 and 2, or black hat and white hat respectively. The video and photographs showed that after the bombs went off, both of these suspects were the ones who had 'acted differently'. While everybody was running for their lives, these two were walking rather 'casually'. They were also found surveying the aftermath of the explosions instead of leaving the blast site immediately.

Upon the release of these pictures and video, the public answered the FBI's call for assistance in identifying them. Different people provided several photographs and records obtained from home movies to the investigators. A deluge of photographs that the police received were in turn scrutinized by the authorities as well as social networks online.

Despite all of these efforts made by both the public and investigators, the suspects still eluded the authorities. The perpetrators were revealed as two brothers whose family had migrated to the United States seeking asylum in 2002. The brothers were identified as 26-year-old

Tamerlan Tsarnaev and 19-year-old Dzhokhar Tsarnaev.

***

Dzhokhar Tsarnaev [18] arrived in the U.S in 2002, along with his parents, while his older brother and two sisters followed them a year later in 2003. Tamerlan Tsarnaev was an amateur boxer who had some early successes in his career before he migrated to the United States. Tamerlan was born in 1986 while Dzhokhar, seven years younger, was born in 1993.

Dzhokhar Tsarnaev

The Tsarnaev family is Muslim and, prior to their immigration, had lived in the Soviet Republic of Kyrgyzstan as well as the Russian republic of Dagestan. Both brothers were born in their native country of Kyrgyzstan. Upon arriving in the United States, the family settled in Cambridge, Massachusetts, and soon applied for political asylum. The brother' father was an ethnic Chechen who had spent most of his life in Kyrgyzstan and their mother was originally from Dagestan.

Tamerlan Tsarnaev

After settling down in the U.S, the father started working as a car mechanic while the mother found work as a facialist. The elder Tsarnaev, Tamerlan, was a community college dropout and had no permanent employment record. He was married and even had a child. He had a green card and was not a naturalized U.S. citizen. It is alleged that he had some charges of battery and assault against him, which is why his citizenship was still pending. During 2011, Tamerlan was even investigated by the Federal Bureau of Investigation who got a tip from Russian officials regarding his involvement in criminal activities. But the officials found no concrete evidence of any activity which could be deemed as incriminating.

On the other hand, Dzhokhar, the younger brother, was different. He was described as a popular student in school by his friends. At the time of the bombings, he was a sophomore at the University of Massachusetts in Dartmouth. He had retained his popularity through college as well and was known to be intelligent and hardworking. According to some accounts, Dzhokhar had even been given a scholarship at school and was looking to pursue a career in medicine.

When their family and friends were questioned about their involvement in the bombings, most of them stated that the Tsarnaev brothers were not particularly religious or radicalized. Upon further research, it was discovered that Tamerlan's views and beliefs had recently undergone a drastic change, just after he recently returned to the US from a trip to Dagestan.

The year following his investigation by the FBI, Tamerlan went to Dagestan and spent six months there. After he returned, he applied for U.S citizenship.

***

The investigators could not come up with any tangible link between the brothers and any terrorist organization. It was later revealed that both of them might have been 'self-radicalized'. Self-radicalization [19] occurs when the person or group that is exhibiting extremist views is not particularly affiliated with any organization or individual. These self-radicalized people usually act upon their own but reflect the ideology and thought of other similar entities.

Similarly, the investigators concluded that while the Tsarnaev brothers were not involved with any organization or other terror plots, they had just developed a militant orientation which had been drawn from disparate sources. Since neither of them had been directly connected to any terrorism activities before the bombings, it was unclear as to what had been the motivation behind the attacks they carried out.

Everyone from the public to the President of the United States wanted to know the motives behind the attacks that led to innocent lives being lost. When President Obama addressed the nation after the bombings, he even raised the question, asking,

"Why did young men who grew up and studied here, as part of our communities and our country, resort to such violence?"

The investigators searched for answers further and discovered that Tamerlan had been running a YouTube channel which had links of many extremist videos that he had shared or posted after his return from Dagestan. It was later revealed that the elder Tsarnaev was also involved in a triple homicide that had occurred in 2011. Investigating officials found evidence that implicated Tamerlan in the triple homicide which took place in Waltham, Massachusetts, during September 2011. One of his associates later confessed about Tamerlan's involvement in the Waltham murders also. He revealed this information during an interrogation by the FBI in May, 2013. "*Brendan Mess, 25, of Waltham; Erik Weissman, 31, of Cambridge; and Raphael Teken, 37, of Cambridge, were discovered dead in Mess's apartment in a two-family house on Sept. 12, 2011. Their throats had been slashed and marijuana was sprinkled on the bodies,*" [20] as reported by the Boston Globe.

Dzhokhar might have been acting under the influence of his brother or was self-radicalized to such an extreme that he chose to jeopardize his life and career. Most of his family and friends had described him as a popular and intelligent person who had a bright future ahead of him. However, when the police caught the younger brother, he revealed during an interrogation that the instructions for the bombs had been obtained by an extremist newsletter which was published by Al-Qaeda.

In a statement, he admitted to building the pressure cooker bombs at home, along with his brother, with the plans obtained from the online newsletter known as *Inspire* and published by the terrorist network in the Arabian Peninsula.

Based on this, the investigators concluded that the younger Tsarnaev had been self-radicalized.

When his friends at college came to know about his involvement in the Boston Marathon attacks, they gathered together in his dorm room and conducted a search. His three friends discovered a backpack containing fireworks, several of them, which had all been emptied of their powder. They decided to throw away the backpack along with all of its contents. It was subsequently recovered and the trio was charged with hindering and misleading the investigation.

***

The FBI investigators were able to conclude that both of the brothers had no roots to any terrorist groups that were known to the authorities. They concluded that the brothers were purely motivated by their extremist religious views. It was further alleged that the Tsarnaev brothers had been considering suicide attacks during the Fourth of July and had other striking places in backup as well. Ultimately they decided to use pressure cooker bombs as those were easier to detonate through a remote control.

Fox News then reported that the attackers chose the marathon to attack due to the 'opportunity' it presented. The prestigious races were a target of opportunity when the building of the bombs were completed much faster than expected.

There were reports stating that Tamerlan was born in the Kalmyk Autonomous Soviet Socialist Republic, North Caucasus, while his other siblings, including Dzhokhar, were born in Kyrgyzstan. Some family accounts claim that Dzokhar was actually born in Dagestan instead of his family's native country. Their family spent some time in Tokmok, Kyrgyzstan and in Makhachkala, Dagestan as well. Through their father, they were half Chechen, while their mother was Avar. It was claimed that although they had never lived in Chechnya, they identified themselves as Chechen. Their family had emigrated to the States seeking refuge from the Chechen conflict, and this might have had an effect on both of the brothers later on.

According to a news article, the brothers were '*avid athletes and good students*'. Tamerlan had been a student at Bunker Hill Community College before he dropped out to become a professional boxer. He aimed to get a spot on the United States Olympic boxing team and had been heard saying that he would 'rather compete' for the United States than Russia, until and unless his native country Chechnya became independent. In 2010, he married an American citizen, Katherine Russell, in a mosque which is situated within the Dorchester area of the city. His wife was pregnant with their daughter at the time of the bombings.

Other claims were brought forward later alleging that Tamerlan had previously stated that he did not understand Americans at all and that none of his friends were Americans. He did not even have one single American friend despite living in the States a long time. His history of violence had also been cited, including an arrest for assault; he had been accused of assaulting his ex-girlfriend in July 2009, for which he was charged.

Meanwhile, Dzhokhar Tsarnaev was

pursuing a major in marine biology at the University of Massachusetts, Dartmouth, when he decided to help his brother with the bomb attacks. He had attained his U.S citizenship in 2012. His brother had been a strong influence in his life, with the younger Tsarnaev even going on record to say that his elder sibling had been the 'driving force' behind the terrorist attack. Dzhokhar admitted that he had been recruited recently by his brother and had agreed to help him with his plan. A news report recorded one of the law enforcement officials saying that the younger Tsarnaev had not appeared as bothered about America's stance and position in the Muslim world as his older brother was. He looked up to his brother and, thus, followed him through. During an interrogation, Dzhokhar is said to have revealed that he and his brother carried out the attacks in retaliation against the United States' role in the Afghanistan and Iraq wars. According to him, the brothers were defending Muslims from the enemy threat posed by the United States.

Furthermore, there was a note that Dzhokhar had written on the inside wall of the boat where he was found hiding. The note, scrawled with a marker by Dzhokhar, said that the Boston Marathon bombs were *'retribution for the United States military action in Afghanistan and Iraq'*. He also referred to the victims of the bombings as *'collateral damage'*, comparing the situation to that of the Muslim world. The interior of the boat where the note had been scribbled was cut out from the hull and presented as evidence in court.

While it may seem like the brothers' motivation behind the attacks were religious, there are some scholars and political analysts who have suggested otherwise. According to these scholars, religion might not have been the primary motive behind the Tsarnaev brothers' involvement in the Boston Marathon bombings. A few of these political analysts even went on record stating that Islam's role in the attacks may have been secondary. In their opinion, the primary motives behind the attacks could have been their family's Chechen background, sympathy towards the political situation within the Caucasus region, or Tamerlan Tsarnaev's inability to relate to the

American culture and society.

The brothers may have been Muslim essentially, but neither of them was very religious or indicated any signs of being radicalized up until a few years ago. Their aunt stated that Tamerlan recently became very devout and strict in his religious beliefs. After 2009, he set up a YouTube channel in his name and started posting a lot of Islamist video links. Investigators also found some political videos in the YouTube playlist regarding the situation in Caucasus.

There were some sources which have reported that, in 2011, the FBI received a tip from the Russian Federal Security Service regarding Tamerlan's radical Islamist views. According to the tip, Tamerlan Tsarnaev had become an extremist Muslim and was following radical Islam. The FBI responded to the tip and launched an investigation into the matter. They ran background checks, searched databases and interviewed all the family members. In the end, the officials decided that the family was not involved with any terrorist network or with any such activity. The investigators had no such evidence that implicated Tamerlan or any other family member in a terrorist activity, either domestic or foreign.

In the following year, 2012, Tamerlan went on a six-month-long visit to Dagestan. It was reported that he made frequent visits to a mosque known for harboring extremism. The Russian Federal Security Service believed that the mosque, situated on Kotrova Street in Makhachkala, was linked to followers of radical Islam. Experts share divided views over this; while many are of the opinion that the radicalization of Tsarvaev brothers occurred at some point in the U.S only, there are others who believe it happened during the trip to Dagestan. Opinions on the subject vary, with some saying that Tamerlan was motivated by his faith as he followed an extremist and anti-American version of Islam, which he turned towards during his time in the country. Political analysts are also of the view that he might have turned to radicalism during his time in Dagestan.

Dzhokhar, on the other hand, had no such aspirations until some time back. His friends and family appeared genuinely shocked upon learning that he had been involved in the bombings. During his interrogation, he himself revealed that his brother had been the mastermind behind the bomb attacks and he had just recently come on board. The younger Tsarnaev had been acting under his brother's influence since both of them were quite close and shared interests. Tamerlan's boxing coach is said to have reported that the younger brother admired his older one greatly and was immensely affected by him.

According to a few analysts and reports, the suspects' mother was known for expressing extremist views and following radical Islam. She had openly supported 'Jihad' some time back and might have been responsible for influencing her sons' behavior. This eventually led to the Russian authorities warning the U.S government regarding the family's actions. The U.S. authorities received two warnings from the Russian officials on different occasions.

Tamerlan and his mother, Zubiedat, had been placed on the terror watch list about eighteen months before the bombing incident occurred. When the FBI was investigating the bombings, they looked into the other Tsarvaev family members as well. They found a girl with the same last name, who turned out to be their sister. Although she had no knowledge about her brothers' involvement in the Boston Marathon attacks, the officials seized computer equipment from her apartment which helped them with the identification of the suspects.

After the pictures and video footage made the rounds, the father of the suspects gave a statement to the FBI officials regarding his sons' involvement. He revealed that his younger son was a sophomore at the University of Massachusetts, Dartmouth, who aspired to pursue a career in medicine.

***

Within hours of the suspects' photos being released to the public, the suspects were involved in the shooting of police officer Sean Collier, 27, [21] on campus at the Massachusetts Institute of Technology. Officer Collier had been on duty at the campus when the suspects targeted him to take his gun.

Collier was seated in his car, which was parked near the Stata Center within the MIT campus. Both of the suspects came to him looking for an extra gun, and when they were unable to get it out of the holster because of its retention system, they shot him six times. These shots proved to be fatal as he was soon pronounced dead after being taken to the Massachusetts General Hospital. One of the law enforcement officers later described the killing as an assassination.

The hunt for the shooter began as investigating officials suspected that the shooting was somehow connected to the

Boston Marathon bombings.

On the other hand, both of the Tsarnaev brothers were on the run. They carjacked a Mercedes-Benz M-Class SUV from a neighborhood in Boston, later revealed as the Allston-Brighton neighborhood. The older brother, Tamerlan, took the owner hostage, threatened him and admitted that he was the culprit behind the Boston attacks as well as the one responsible for the death of the police officer. Dzhokhar was not with him in the Mercedes; he followed in a green Honda and joined his brother later in the car. This Honda actually led to his identification by the investigators after it was found abandoned. (It was later learned during the interrogation that both of the brothers had made a spontaneous decision to leave for New York and carry out similar bomb attacks in Times Square.)

Both of the brothers forced the hostage to use his ATM card to obtain cash. They stopped at various locations, collecting over eight hundred dollars cash until the daily withdrawal limit ran out. The brothers then split up, with one of them driving the Mercedes while the other one followed in his Honda Civic. An all-points bulletin was issued by United States authorities for the Honda, which had been marked by the investigators as being a suspicious vehicle.

The car's owner, referred to as Danny in early reports, was actually a Chinese man named Dun Meng. He barely managed to escape when the suspects stopped for a refill at a gas station; he somehow freed himself and ran to another gas station nearby. Once he got there, he asked a clerk to call for help. The clerk in turn called 911, and soon the police arrived on the scene. By that time, the suspects had already taken off. However, Meng's cellphone still remained in their vehicle which helped the police track the car down. Investigators and police officials were able to focus their search based on the location of the cellphone. Within a few hours, they were able to track the phone and the vehicle to Watertown.

***

On April 19, shortly after midnight, a police officer from Watertown was able to identify the brothers in the Honda and the stolen Mercedes-Benz SUV. Joseph

Reynolds, the officer who identified the suspects, notified the other police officers who began arriving on the scene. Just minutes after the police began to make a move on the suspects at large, shots were fired. [22]

A full-fledged gunfight broke out, resulting in a standoff between the police and the brothers around the 100 block of Laurel Street. According to estimates, around two hundred to three hundred rounds of ammunition were fired that night, along with a bomb and several crude grenades being thrown at the police.

The Watertown Police Chief gave a statement later, in which he said that the brothers had an entire arsenal of guns and grenades. According to him, the older Tsarvaev brother, Tamerlan, upon running out of ammunition, was tackled and caught by the police. At the same time, the younger brother, Dzhokhar, came towards the police driving the SUV at full speed. While the police officers escaped with minor injuries, Tamerlan, his brother, was run over. The SUV dragged him down the street for a short distance as it drove away. Dzhokhar sped on ahead, without stopping, until he came across the corner of Spruce and Lincoln Streets. He stopped at the corner which was almost half a mile away from the location of the shootout.

His car was found abandoned there, while he had escaped on foot. When the police searched the scene, they found one single gun with a defaced serial number. The firearm was revealed to be a Ruger 9mm pistol. The police took custody of the pistol and fired several rounds all over the area. In ten minutes, the place looked like a battle ground, with several houses nearby bearing bullet holes.

Tamerlan Tsarnaev, gravely injured after being run over by the SUV, was transported to a nearby hospital where he was pronounced dead. The Beth Israel Deaconess Medical Center admitted Tamerlan whereupon a medical team tried to resuscitate him, but they were unsuccessful, and he died at 1:35 a.m. on April 19.

On the death certificate, the cause of death reads, '*gunshot wounds to the torso and extremities, blunt trauma to the head and torso*'. The certificate also recounted his being shot by the police, being run over and dragged by a vehicle, all three of which contributed to his death. According to officials, he had been killed by his own brother. His death was also ruled as a homicide.

The firefight rendered a MBTA Police officer severely wounded. It was revealed afterwards that Richard H. Donohue Jr., 33, had been critically wounded by what was deemed friendly fire. He was admitted to Mount Auburn Hospital with a gaping bullet wound to the thigh and extreme loss of blood which had put his life in danger. Fortunately, he survived. There were fifteen other police officers who suffered minor injuries from the shootings and explosions that occurred during the firefight.

A report of sixty-plus pages was produced by the Harvard Kennedy School's Program on Crisis Leadership which analyzed the firefight and manhunt in detail. [23] According to that report, there was a lack of co-ordination between the police department and law enforcement agencies which had exposed the public to excessive risk at the time of the shootout.

***

After the Watertown incident, the FBI officials released more photos of the two suspects in order to catch Dzhokhar. On April 19, early in the day, the residents of Watertown received reverse 911 calls, requesting people to stay indoors. Come mid-morning, the Governor made an official announcement, asking all the residents of Watertown, as well as those in adjacent towns and cities, to stay inside. Panic ensued as the residents of Boston, Brookline, Belmont, Allston-Brighton, Cambridge, Waltham, and Newton were given a '*shelter in place*' [24] order. It was later lifted by the Governor in the evening, after the manhunt came up empty.

Residents of Somerville were also given a 'shelter in place' order. A twenty-block area in Watertown was cordoned off by the police officers and residents were asked to stay in and not answer their doors, no matter what. The area was then scoured by officers in tactical gear. SWAT teams were present on scene with armored vehicles, moving through in a single formation with their officers going through every nook and corner. Helicopters circled the area, prepared to apprehend the suspect in case he was found on the scene.

Apart from all this, present on the location were FBI officials, the Department of Homeland Security, Bureau of Alcohol, Firearms and Explosives, Boston and Watertown Police Departments, the National Guard, and Massachusetts State Police officers. This show of all forces was the first time on field for the inter-agency task force that had been created after the 9/11 attacks to deal with such emergencies.

Boston's entire public transit network was suspended, along with its taxi service. Even the Amtrak service which operated to and from the city was put on hold. The Logan International Airport authorities announced that they were going to remain operational; however, security around the area was heightened. Businesses, schools and universities were all shut down as security personnel and hundreds of law enforcement officers conducted an unprecedented manhunt, going door to door in Watertown.

Other leads were followed as well; the house that both the brothers had shared was located in Cambridge, and it was raided by the police officers in search of the suspect. While he still eluded the authorities, seven other improvised explosive devices were recovered from the house.

The brothers' father, who at the time was in Makhachkala, Dagestan, gave a statement from his home there. He appealed to his son to surrender and 'give up'. He addressed his son, asking him to, 'give up and come home to Russia.' He also said that if the authorities killed him, 'all hell would break loose'. Dzhokhar Tsarnaev's uncle, who lived in Montgomery Village, Maryland, also came on television and pleaded that he turn himself in.

At around 6 p.m. on the evening of April 19, the 'shelter in place' orders were lifted, and two hours later, the manhunt also came to an end. Just outside the area that had been cordoned off during the search, a local resident went to his backyard and noticed that the cover of the boat kept there was loose. Upon close observation, he found that a body was lying under the cover, inside the boat, and there was a pool of blood surrounding it.

He immediately alerted the police who responded by arriving on the scene promptly. The boat was surrounded by several officers who started verifying the movement of the body through a forward-looking infrared thermal imaging device that was being operated from a State Police helicopter. As soon as the suspect started to move around the tarp of the boat, the police officers opened fire. The gunfire went on until the Superintendent stepped up and ordered a ceasefire.

The authorities announced Dzhokhar's capture, and America celebrated. Thousands of citizens took to the streets of Massachusetts to celebrate the capture that had occurred after a tense day that saw a number of cities and towns on complete lockdown.

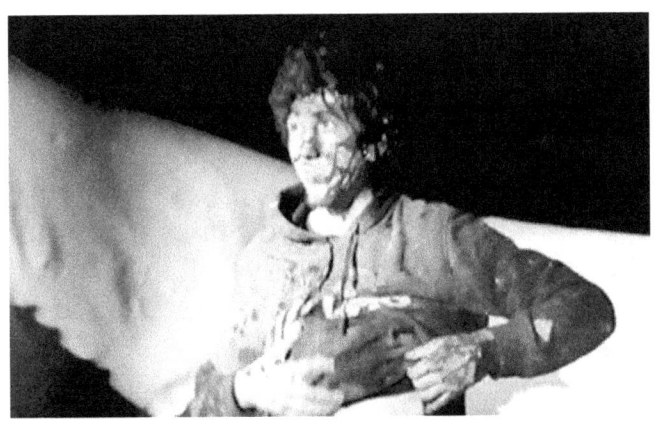

Initial reports by the police stated that Dzhokhar was in possession of a firearm and had shot several times at the police officers during the final confrontation. It was clarified later that the suspect had no weapon of any kind on him when he was captured. At 8:42 p.m., he was taken into custody and transported to the Beth Israel Deaconess Medical Center. His condition at the time was listed as critical due to several gunshot wounds to the face, neck, head, hands and legs. It was first believed that the gunshot wound on the neck was a result of a possible suicide attempt, but this was contradicted by the revelation that he had been unarmed at the time of his capture. Later on, some of the

SWAT team members described the gunshot wound on the neck as a slicing injury that could have been possibly caused by shrapnel from the earlier explosions.

***

A number of United States Senators, along with a Representative of the House, put forth the suggestion that Dzhokhar should be tried as an 'unlawful enemy combatant' and not as a criminal. This could potentially prevent him from claiming his right to legal counsel. There were other sources and lawmakers who opposed this suggestion and were of the opinion that trying him as an enemy combatant would be illegal and could possibly jeopardize the prosecution.

The United States government made a decision to try the captured bomber in federal criminal court and not as an unlawful enemy combatant.

Dzhokhar Tsarnaev was interrogated for sixteen hours by the investigators and communicated with them throughout. However, on April 22, he went silent and stopped all communications with them. The reason behind his silence was believed to be

Judge Marianna Bowler's reading of his Miranda rights. Investigators were of the opinion that after he was read the Miranda rights, he decided to stay silent and not respond to their questions. Previously, before the interrogation had started, Dzhokhar had not been given a Miranda warning since the officials from the federal law enforcement agencies invoked the public safety exception to the rights.

This action by the law enforcement officials started a debate as questions were raised regarding the admission of his statements in court. Many people were not sure whether or not Dzhokhar's statement would be admissible in court as evidence.

***

Formal charges were brought against Dzhokhar Tsarnaev on April 22, 2013. The United States District Court for the District of Massachusetts officially invoked charges upon him during a bedside hearing which was held at the time he was hospitalized. He was charged with usage of weapons of mass destruction as well as a malicious destruction of property that led to loss of life. A few of the charges against him carried the possibility of life imprisonment or even the death penalty.

The court found Tsarnaev to be mentally competent and alert during the hearing. He was responsive to the questions and lucid, although he answered most of the questions by nodding his head. When the Judge asked whether he would be able to afford legal counsel, his reply was that he couldn't afford it. He was then assigned and represented by Federal Public Defenders.

On April 26, Dzhokhar was transferred from the Beth Israel Deaconess Medical Center to the Federal Medical Center at Fort Devens, which is more than forty miles away from Boston. The Federal Medical Center is a medical facility of the federal prison, established at an old army base. He was kept in solitary confinement within an isolated housing unit that was kept on a twenty-three hour lockdown.

Dzhokhar made his first public appearance in court on July 10, 2013, and he pled not guilty to all thirty of the charges made against him, including the one for murder of a MIT police officer. He reappeared in court on September 23 for a status hearing, during which his lawyers put in a request for more time to prepare a defense. Two weeks later, his attorneys requested the court to lift the special administrative measures which were imposed on the suspect in custody by Attorney General Holder. The lawyers stated that these measures had isolated Tsarnaev and cut off all his communication with family, friends and legal counsel. They argued that there had been no evidence of him posing any threat in the future, hence, the restriction on him in prison should be eased.

***

On September 24, 2014, Judge George O'Toole, ruled that the trial of Dzhokhar Tsarnaev would begin by January 5, 2015, two months later than the expected date. The reason for the delay was the extensive evidence that had to be observed and scrutinized by both the defense and prosecutor. He also stated that the motion filed by defense for an elongated delay was unwarranted, so the trial could not be pushed to September 25, 2015, as desired by Dzhokhar's attorneys.

Furthermore, the defense had also failed to prove their claim that the media coverage of the matter would lead to '*an inflamed and pervasively prejudiced potential area jury pool*'. The request for change of venue to Washington, D.C., was put forth by Dzhokar's lawyers on the basis that a '*fair and impartial jury could not be impaneled in the district*'.

Judge O'Toole denied this request as well, ruling that no such evidence had been brought forward to support this claim either.

Tsarnaev reappeared in public for the first time after July 2013 when he attended his first pretrial hearing which was held on December 18, 2014.

Jury selection for the trial started in January with almost 1,373 prospective jurors filling out the questionnaires in the initial pool. By the end of February, Judge O'Toole, the prosecutors and the defense team agreed to settle on a pool of 70 jury prospects. These prospective jury members had been narrowed down after 256 people were questioned during individual interviews that were scheduled over 21 days.

The final jury was selected on March 3, 2015, and consisted of 10 women and 8 men. On March 4, the trial officially began with opening statements from both sides being presented in court. The Assistant U.S Attorney spoke for the prosecution and, in his statement, described the scene of the bombing vividly. According to him, Dzhokhar was equally guilty of the crime as his brother was and had been on a mission against Americans.

On the other hand, the defense made an opening statement which was directed at saving Dzhokhar from the death penalty. The lawyer did agree that he had been present at all the crime scenes, including the Watertown shootout, during the murder of Officer Sean Collier and the carjacking incident. However, he had acted under the influence of his brother, and all his actions indicated that he had been following the older Tsarnaev.

The trial went on until March 30 during which the prosecution called almost 90 witnesses and recorded their testimony over a course of 15 days. The prosecution brought some injured victims of the bombings to the stand, who recounted all the panic and chaos that had occurred during the day. A few of them who had lost their limbs, as a result of direct impact from the explosions, gave detailed accounts of their wounds and amputations.

On March 31, the following day, the defense also finished presenting their side of the case in the guilt phase after calling a total of 4 witnesses to the stand.

Closing arguments from both sides were presented on April 6. Two days later, a verdict was reached and Tsarnaev was found guilty on all accounts. There were 30 charges against him, including murder, conspiracy, bombing and possession of weapons of mass destruction. Out of these 30 charges, 17 carried the possibility of a death penalty.

On April 21, the sentencing phase of the trial began and a verdict was reached on May 15. It took the American public by utter surprise with many of them expressing shock over the court's decision. Dzhokhar Tsarnaev was sentenced to death by lethal injection.

Tsarnaev was officially sentenced to death on June 24, 2015, after he had issued a formal apology to the victims of the Boston Marathon bombings.

Author's Note - *"Out of the 80 federal defendants sentenced to death in the last 27 years, only 3 have been executed. With appeals, Tsarnaev may remain in prison for decades at a cost of $165,000 per year of tax-payer's money to feed, guard and shelter him."*

The Fort Hood Shootings

A mass shooting occurred on November 5, 2009, at Fort Hood, Texas. Fort Hood, an American military base near Killeen, Texas, became the target of a mass shooting that saw thirteen people killed and more than thirty injured. The perpetrator of the crime was a U.S Army major and a psychiatrist. [25]

Nidal Hasan was caught and subdued by the officers on scene and immediately took credit as being the shooter. This shooting produced the highest number of casualties on an American military base as a result of terrorism. During the shooting, Hasan also took a bullet which left him paralyzed.

His trial took place in 2011, while his court martial started during 2013. He was charged on thirteen murder counts and thirty-two attempted murders. In August 2013, he was officially sentenced to death. Later it was revealed that he had ties to an

Islamist radical group and was increasingly becoming radicalized himself. The victims of the attacks were awarded the Purple Heart [26], as well as its civilian equivalent, by the Army, to commemorate their bravery.

Nidal Hasan

***

It is believed that Hasan started planning the shooting during July 2009. His preparation began when he went to the Guns Galore store, located in Killeen, on July 31. The information was revealed during pretrial testimony which also stated that Hasan purchased a FN Five-Seven Semi-automatic pistol from the store.

Army Specialist, William Gilbert, later revealed that Hasan walked into the store and asked to see the 'most technologically advanced weapon' available in the market. He also required a weapon that possessed the 'highest standard magazine capacity'. This Army Specialist, a regular customer at the store, was present at the time when Hasan entered and asked to see the weapon that he would later use in the shooting at Fort Hood.

In fact, the Specialist was one of the three people who recommended the FN Five-seven gun to Hasan. The store manager, along with an employee, also described the functions and operation of the pistol to him in detail. However, Hasan did not buy the weapon on that same day. He left the store at the time, saying that he still needed to do some research on the recommended pistol. But he returned to the store the following day and bought the FN Five-seven pistol. After that, he would return to the store once every week and buy extra magazines. Along with these extra magazines, he bought more than three thousand rounds of 5.7x28mm and SS197SR ammunition. During the weeks before the attacks, Hasan started going to an outdoor shooting range, situated in Florence, where he used to practice with the weapon. Supposedly, he became quite a marksman, hitting silhouette targets up to a distance of a hundred yards.

***

The Soldier Readiness Processing Center, Hasan's workplace, is a facility where army personnel undergo routine medical treatment and physical fitness tests, just before and upon return from deployment. Hasan checked into the center on November 5, 2009, at approximately 1:43 p.m.

He had armed himself with the FN Five-seven pistol to which he had made some modifications as well. The pistol had been fitted with a couple of laser sights (LaserMax); one was green and the other red. Later on, it was discovered that Hasan also had another weapon on him, a Smith and Wesson .375 Magnum revolver. However, the revolver had not been used to shoot anybody on the scene.

An eyewitness later stated that, when Hasan walked in the facility, nothing about him seemed suspicious. He took an empty seat at a table and sat there with his head bowed for quite a few minutes. All of a sudden, he stood up, loudly yelled 'Allahu Akbar' (*Islamic phrase meaning 'God is greater'*), and started shooting.

Hasan opened fire relentlessly, moving in a 'fanlike' motion initially, spraying bullets everywhere. He then started targeting the soldiers individually, taking shots at them over and over again. According to an eyewitness, a sergeant at the scene, the rate of the gunshots fired was quite steady and 'pretty much constant'. When he heard the shooting as it started, he thought the sound was something like an M16.

John Gaffaney, an Army Reserve Captain, charged at Hasan in an attempt to stop him but was mortally wounded in his attempt and was unable to get to Hasan.

Michael Cahill, a civilian physical assistant, also made a charge at the shooter by throwing a chair his way in an attempt to stop him. He did not succeed and was shot and killed. Another Army Reserve Specialist, Logan Burnett, threw a folding table towards Hasan, but that did not stop him either. Hasan moved forward, shooting Burnett and wounding him critically. Burnett survived as the bullet hit him in his left hip, after which he fell to the ground and was able to crawl towards a cubicle close by.

The reason all these soldiers were not firing back at the shooter was because the base was a gun-free zone. Unbelievable that trained military personnel were left helpless without the weapons and tools they are trained to use. But one of President Bill Clinton's first acts upon taking office in 1993 was "to disarm U.S. soldiers on military bases." In March 1993, the Army imposed regulations forbidding military personnel from carrying their personal firearms and making it almost impossible for commanders to issue firearms to soldiers in the U.S. for personal protection.

Eyewitnesses also testified that Hasan deliberately targeted the soldiers in uniform. Although there were several civilians on the scene, he passed up all opportunities to shoot at them, instead targeting only the soldiers.

During his trial, witnesses described the incident wherein Hasan came face to face with a group of civilians hiding under a desk. Reportedly, he walked towards them but did not fire a single shot. The laser sight dot of his pistol moved across one man's face as Hasan looked upon the civilians under the desk. However, he simply turned around and walked away from them without shooting anybody.

Sergeant Kimberly Munley, base civilian police, immediately rushed to the site in her patrol car. She encountered Hasan Nidal right outside the area in front of the Soldier Readiness Processing Center. Hasan fired at Officer Munley, who in turn shot back at him, using the 9mm M9 she had with her. Her bullets failed to stop him while she took three hits and was gravely injured. Two of her injuries were from gun shot wounds, one of which hit her thigh and the other struck her knee. As she was beginning to fall to the ground after being hit by the first bullet, a second shot was fired at her. That second bullet struck and shattered her femur, after which she fell to the ground and lost consciousness. She suffered wounds to her hand, as it was struck by shrapnel, when one of the bullets Hasan fired at her hit a rain gutter nearby.

Hasan then walked up to her and kicked her gun out of reach. He kept on moving forward, firing at the soldiers and police officers. While the shootings continued outside, nursing staff and paramedics rushed inside the building to help the injured victims. They were able to secure the area off with a belt and provide aid to the victims. However, many members of the nursing staff recounted a lot of difficulties that they faced on scene. It looked like a battleground, with blood everywhere and bodies riddled with bullet holes.

Since there was so much blood on the ground, the nursing staff and the medics found it very hard to get across to the injured. They had difficulties in maintaining a balance and getting medical aid to all the wounded people in need of it immediately.

As the nurses and medics were helping the people inside, Hasan continued with his shooting spree within the area outside the center. He targeted the soldiers who were fleeing from his line of fire, and then moved on to the police officers who had responded to the shootout at the facility. The area was soon surrounded by civilian police officers as backup was dispatched to the scene and more of them reached the site. One of the officers who had arrived on scene, Sergeant Mark Todd, confronted Hasan and commanded him to surrender. In his statement later on, Todd stated that "*When I shouted at Hasan to drop his gun and surrender, he did not say a word back. Instead he just turned around and fired. After shooting a couple of rounds at me, Hasan began to move forward.*"

However, Todd fired back and the two exchanged shots. Eventually the civilian police officer was able to subdue Hasan, taking him down with five shots. He acted very quickly, slapped the handcuffs on him, and kicked the pistol out of his reach as he hit the ground and fell unconscious.

Todd described him as 'calm' and 'methodical' during the shootout. Hasan had taken to hiding behind a telephone pole and shooting his fellow soldiers 'in the back' as they fled from the scene. He kept on firing at the soldiers as they ran to hide and seek shelter from the rampant bullets. This was when Todd confronted him and took him down. Reportedly, he flinched when he was shot and still clutched on to his pistol with the laser sight on it as he slid down the pole. The officer ran up to him and kicked the pistol away.

Officer Todd could tell that he was 'breathing'; he didn't say anything as he faded out but just kept on 'blinking'.

Hasan's colleagues later spoke about his continuous outbursts regarding religion and extremism. His long talks also carried extremist views and talk on religion instead of medical issues. His fellow doctors later reported that Hasan Nidal had openly claimed that he was a 'Muslim first and American second'. One of the Army doctors even said that he did not file a complaint against him due to fear of appearing discriminatory against Muslims.

A neighbor of Hasan's went on record to say that, on the morning of that fateful day, just before he went on to the Army base, Hasan gave her a Koran and said, "I'm going to do good work for God".

The incident sent shockwaves, not just through America, but across the globe as well. An Army base in the United States had been attacked, leaving thirteen dead and thirty severely injured. Although the shootings were not labeled as an act of terrorism at the time, the Senators, lawmakers and the President of the United States called it a terrorist attack.

The victims of the shootings were honored with medals of bravery conferred by the Army and the government. Many of those who had suffered grave injuries were civilian police officers, who were commended by the government and the victims' families for their service to the country and its people. Hasan was taken into custody and moved to a hospital where he was placed under twenty-four surveillance. He had been shot four times and one of the bullets had hit his spine. He failed to recover from that injury and became a paraplegic.

During the investigation, it was discovered that Hasan had expressed his radicalized Islamist views on a number of occasions; lawmakers speculated that those views might have possibly motivated him into carrying out the attack.

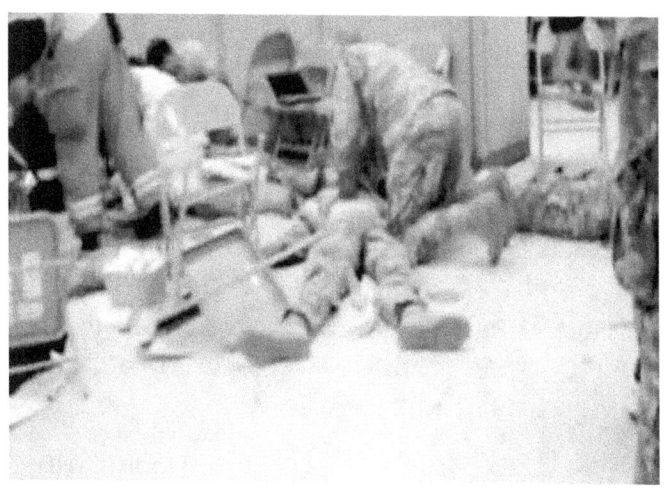

Cahill Caraveo DeCrow Gaffaney Greene Krueger Nemelka

Hunt Pearson Seager Velez Warman Xiong

13 Victims of the Fort Hood Shooting

***

After Hasan was caught, an investigation regarding the incident and its proceedings was launched. The scene was surveyed and every detail was analyzed. According to one of the investigators, one-hundred-and-forty-six spent shell casings were found and recovered from inside the building. Officials also found and collected sixty-eight shell casings around the area outside the Center. A total of two-hundred-and-fourteen rounds were fired between the terrorist and police.

The medic who treated Hasan after

he was taken into custody, stated that upon going through his pockets, he discovered that they were filled with pistol magazines. In fact, almost two hundred unspent rounds were on Hasan's person. The ammunition was both in thirty- and twenty-round magazines and initially led witnesses to believe that there might have been more than one shooter involved in the incident.

The overall shooting incident went on for ten minutes and led to the death of thirteen people, out of which twelve were soldiers and one was a civilian. Eleven were so badly wounded that they died at the scene, while two were taken to a hospital nearby where they couldn't be resuscitated and were pronounced dead. Over thirty people were seriously injured, some bearing multiple bullet wounds, and were rushed to various hospitals in the area.

In initial reports, many speculated that there were a total of three soldiers involved in the shooting. It led to the investigators detaining two other soldiers for questioning. They were subsequently released after no evidence was found connecting them to the shooting.

The shootout at Fort Hood put the Army and the counter-terrorism departments on alert throughout the country. Just immediately after the shooting was over, and Hasan was taken into custody, Fort Hood base and other surrounding areas were ordered to be on lockdown. The military police along with the U.S Army Criminal Investigation Command monitored the areas on lockdown and were on a heavy guard until about 7:00 that evening. Apart from this, the Texas DPS troopers, Texas Rangers, deputy officers from the Bell County Sheriff Department and the FBI officials from Waco and Austin were ordered to the Fort Hood Army base. The United States President, Barack Obama, was immediately briefed on the incident and would later make a statement regarding the attack.

***

A year later, on November 5, 2010, fifty-two injured victims of the shooting incident received commendations and awards honoring their acts of bravery during the shootout. Captain John Gaffaney, the soldier who died trying to stop the shooter by throwing a chair his way, was awarded the Soldier's Medal posthumously. Fifty more medals were awarded to responders and soldiers for their bravery and quick actions that restricted the number of casualties on scene. Seven of these soldiers were conferred with the 'Soldier's Medal', presented by the Secretary of the Army and Fort Hood's Commanding General.

The civilian police officers, Kimberly Munley and Sergeant Mark Todd, both of whom played a crucial role in stopping the shooter, were awarded the Secretary of the Army Award for Valor for their actions. Another civilian, physical assistant Michael Cahill, was presented the award posthumously. On May 23, 2011, he was conferred with the Army Award for Valor posthumously for his bravery. Cahill died during an attempt to charge at Hasan using a folding chair.

In May 2012, the US Senate and Congress agreed to pass a bill which proposed a legislation allowing the victims of the shootings to be awarded the Purple Heart. The Congress held its 113th session, in which Representative John Carter announced the new legislation to change the designation of the shooting. It went from being 'workplace violence' to 'combat related'. According to the National Defense Authorization Act, this broadened the criteria for conferring the Purple Heart upon the victims. It would now include those who suffered from a direct attack by a terrorist organization or from an attack which was 'inspired or motivated by terrorist or foreign terror group'.

The awards were handed out on April 10, 2015, to all the survivors of the attacks.

***

There were thirteen people who died from bullet wounds or from impact as a result of hitting the ground. The thirty people who were wounded received injuries from bullets, shrapnel and falls incurred during the shootout. Many of them suffered from psychological trauma and shock long after the incident had occurred.

Hasan Nidal was taken to the Scott and White Memorial Hospital, which is a trauma center located in Temple, Texas. Nidal was later moved to San Antonio, Texas, where he was admitted in the Brooke Army Medical Center. He was placed under heavy guard and constant surveillance within the facility.

He had suffered four gunshot wounds, one of which left him paralyzed from the waist down. After his discharge from the hospital, he was held within the Bell County Jail, Belton, Texas.

The thirteen people who were slain as a result of the shooting were mostly soldiers. Michael Grant Cahill was the only civilian casualty, being the civilian physical assistant present on scene during the shooting. The victims ranged from a Lieutenant Colonel to Private First Class soldier, all between the ages of sixty-two and nineteen. Cahill was the oldest victim, being sixty-two-years-old, while the youngest victim was nineteen-year-old Private First Class Aaron Thomas Nemelka. Among the dead were Private First Class Francheska Velez, twenty-one years old, who was pregnant when she was shot in the chest. Her baby also died with her.

A list of thirty people, containing a record of all the injured, was released by investigating officials. There were Specialists, Sergeants, Staff Sergeants and other officers who suffered from bullet wounds in the arms, legs, torsos and hips. They all survived after receiving medical aid on scene and treatment at the hospitals later. However, most of the victims suffered from trauma and shock later on. Some of them were able to recover quickly, with eight of these injured soldiers being deployed overseas on November 20, 2009.

***

Nidal's court martial was held on August 6, 2013, before a panel of thirteen Army Officers. During the court martial, Major Hasan Nidal [27] declared that he was indeed the shooter of the Fort Hood incident.

It was revealed during his investigation that Hasan was unmarried with no known partners or current relationships. He was also fairly anti-social, with some people describing him as socially isolated. Hasan was born in the United States. He was a practicing Muslim who became more pious and devout in his beliefs after the death of his parents. According to one of his cousins, his parents passed away in 1998 and 2001 respectively, and their deaths led to the transformation in Hasan's religious beliefs. He became a more devoted Muslim and started keeping to himself. However, his cousin clarified that, at the time, there was no anti-American sentiment in Hasan's views, and neither did he express any extremist thought.

Another cousin, Nader Hasan, a lawyer from Virginia, was of the opinion that Hasan Nidal turned against America after treating patients and hearing their stories of the war in Afghanistan and Iraq. He told some members of his family that he wanted to leave the military as he did not want to work for an Army fighting against Muslims. His anguish against the military was deepening, yet he stayed with them as he said that he was unable to leave his position there.

He was stationed at the Walter Reed Medical Center during the time of his residency and internship, from 2003 to 2009. In 2009, he also completed a two-year fellowship at USUHS. The National Public Radio reported that several officials at the Walter Reed Medical Center repeatedly expressed concerns about Hasan's behavior. During his six-year tenure there, his fellow colleagues had a number of complaints regarding his outbursts and religious talk during medical sessions. However, his colleagues never formally filed any complaints against him for fear it would appear as discrimination.

Hasan's supervisors were also not satisfied with his work, giving him poor evaluation reports and warning him about his substandard performance. During 2008, and even later, a number of meetings between the key officials at the Walter Reed Center took place, where they all discussed Hasan Nidal and how to handle him. Among those key officials who attended those meetings were the Chief of Psychiatry at Walter Reed Center, chairman of the USUHS Department of Psychiatry, another psychiatrist, the director of the Walter Reed psychiatry residency program, and two assistant chairs belonging to the USUHS Department of Psychiatry. One of the assistant chairs from USUHS was the director of Hasan Nidal's fellowship in psychiatry. Accordingly, his fellow colleagues and faculty members were very concerned and 'deeply troubled' by his behavior.

He had been described as 'aloof', 'belligerent', 'paranoid', and possibly suffering from a schizoid personality disorder. At one time when he was giving a lecture to the other psychiatrists, instead of talking about medical issues, he picked up a religious topic. He told the audience that the Koran is very clear about the punishment given to all non-believers. Those who were among them would go to hell or be set on fire, have burning oil poured inside them, and would even be decapitated afterwards. Another Muslim psychiatrist, sitting in the audience, rose up and spoke against Hasan's claim. His stance was that Islam or the Koran on no such occasion has stated this against anybody and Hasan was quoting things out of context or had misinterpreted the Islamic teachings.

In another lecture, Hasan expressed support for 'Jihad' and justified suicide bombings.

Nidal was transferred to Fort Hood in 2009, after he had completed all of his programs. Once at Fort Hood, he rented an apartment in a slightly rundown area, away from all the other officers at the base. Just two days before he went on his shooting spree, Hasan gave away all of his furniture from the apartment. He cited deployment as a reason behind moving out. His neighbors said that he handed out copies of the Koran, Muslim Holy Book, and his business cards which had a Maryland contact number printed upon them. The card read: Behavioral Sciences-Mental Health-Life Skills. Nidal Hasan, MD, MPH. SoA (SWT), Psychiatrist. His business cards did not state his rank.

Later, as the investigators started retracing the steps of the shooter back to where it all began, they found more information about Hasan's turn to radicalism.

In May 2001, Hasan went to his mother's funeral which was held in Falls Church, Virginia, at Dar Al-Hijra Mosque. The Mosque has over three thousand members. Officials speculated that he may have prayed there on earlier occasions as well. Before becoming a member of the mosque in Virginia, Hasan had been a regular attendee at the Muslim Community Center in Silver Spring, Maryland. For a period of ten years, he visited the Center many times a week to offer his prayers there. It was much closer to his residence and workplace.

The imam (leader of the congregation) and members at the Center regularly saw him there until he moved towards the Falls Church mosque.

It has been reported that when he started attending the mosque in Falls Church, Virginia, he may have had run-ins with two of the hijackers involved in the September 11 attacks. His attendance at the mosque was at the same time when Hani Hanjour and Najaf al-Hazmi were also going there regularly. These two were the hijackers, later found to be the perpetrators of the 9/11 attacks, and had been visiting the Falls Church mosque from April to late summer in 2001.

One law enforcement officer on the investigation stated that "*the FBI will be conducting further research on this matter and will look deeper into the claim that Hasan had links with the September 11 terrorists.*"

Upon review, it was revealed that Hasan Nidal did visit with an Islamist radical prior to the shooting and communicated with him via email as well. A law enforcement officer came forward with the report, saying that Hasan's computer and email accounts provided them with evidence regarding the matter.

This Islamist radical turned out to be Anwar-al-Awlaki, who was the imam at the mosque in Falls Church, Virginia, where Hasan had recently started going. He had held the position of the imam at the Dar Al-Hijra Mosque from 2000 to 2002 and was reportedly involved in sheltering the 9/11 hijackers. It turned out that Al-Awlaki had been investigated by the FBI a number of times and was responsible for helping the hijackers get settled and was known for giving extremist speeches at the mosque. Hanjour and al-Hazmi had been spiritually guided by Al-Awlaki when he met them at a mosque in San Diego, and they kept in touch with him even after going to the East Coast.[28]

It was revealed that Hasan had been an admirer of Al-Awlaki and was influenced by his teachings. The imam had been put under surveillance after 2006, before which he was considered to be fairly moderate in his views. Hasan had communicated with the imam and over twenty emails had been exchanged between them between December 2008 and June 2009. These emails raised a red flag with the Feds, and Hasan was eventually investigated by the FBI regarding the subject of his emails.

During a press release issued by FBI officials and investigators of the case on November 9, 2009, it was discovered that Hasan had 'certain communications' with someone who the Joint Terrorism Task Force had under surveillance. As part of their investigation and probe, the Task Force had highlighted those emails and notified the FBI about Hasan. Media reports after the shooting incident stated the 'communications' were emails and that the recipient of those was indeed, Al-Awlaki.

In one of the emails that were exchanged between the two, Hasan wrote, "*I can't wait to join you in the afterlife*". A military analyst, working at the Center for Advanced Defense Studies, analyzed his email and suggested that it could mean one of two things: either Hasan had already decided to offer himself up in the way of religion or he was offering to commit to the cause. Officials said that his other emails were also of a similar nature; he inquired about 'Jihad', how it was appropriate and when to participate in it.

The FBI and military both were informed about his emails from before. When the Army personnel were informed about his contacts, they thought that all those emails were part of his research. Hasan had been researching on professional mental health regarding Muslims in the armed forces, and hence, the Army believed that all his communication was consistent with his master's program in Disaster and Preventive Psychiatry.

There was a joint terrorism task force operating under the FBI and based in DC that was brought in on the matter. One of its employees, belonging to the Defense Criminal Investigative Service, reviewed and analyzed all of the information. After conducting extensive inquiry, the employee concluded that the information was limited and not enough to launch a bigger investigation on both of the subjects. Thus, the matter rested for the time being.

Further on, senior officials belonging to the Department of Defense revealed that their department had no knowledge of those investigations prior to the shooting at Fort Hood.

***

After the shooting, when Hasan had been taken into custody and his trial was pending, a number of analysts started debating his possible motives behind the shooting. Government officials and investigators discussed his psychological state before he went on the shooting spree. According to one of the psychologists, Hasan's colleagues in the psychiatry department had failed to recognize that someone in their midst was so deeply disturbed.

Another official, commenting on his background, stated that Hasan was pending deployment to Afghanistan near the end of November, and he was possibly upset about that. It could have been one of the reasons why he went on this rampage against the military. Later on, Hasan's aunt, Noel Hammad, gave a statement saying that nobody in Hasan's family was aware about his possible deployment to Afghanistan.

According to a report in the Dallas Morning News, some new information regarding Hasan's employment background had come to light. The report referenced an ABC News statement that investigators might have found a possible motive behind the shooter's actions, that it could possibly be related to his patients. The investigators suspected that the shooting could have been triggered by the fact that Hasan's superior refused to process his requests about prosecuting some of his patients for war crimes. Hasan forwarded any requests to his superiors, asking them to look into his patients and prosecute them, based on their statements made during the psychiatry sessions.

Patrick McLain, an attorney and Marine, stated that "*Hasan's request may have been justified legally, but no further comment could be made without researching those sessions with his patients. His superiors and fellow psychiatrists responded to these reports by clarifying that Hasan's requests could not be processed as they were in violation of the doctor-patient confidentiality agreement.*"

Hasan had been mentoring a recent convert to Islam, Duane Reasoner. He had been learning more about the religion from him and, hence, was familiar with his views. In a statement he gave later, Reasoner said that Hasan was not ready to be deployed to Afghanistan. His stance was that Muslims should not be in the United States Military, since it was wrong for Muslims to kill fellow Muslims. Hasan even told Reasoner to avoid joining the military service as it was not the right place to be for him as a Muslim.

The chairman of the Senate Committee on Homeland Security and Governmental Affairs, Senator Joe Lieberman, called for further research into the matter. He said that as for now it was 'premature' to come to any conclusions regarding Hasan's motive behind the shootings. He said that the Army and FBI officials should be allowed to investigate further before any conclusions can be reached. Just two weeks later, when Lieberman opened the Committee's hearing, he referred to the Fort Hood attack as *"the most destructive attack on America since the events of September 11, 2001."*

A renowned forensic psychiatrist, Dr. Michael Welner, M.D, who had prior experience analyzing mass shootings, was of the opinion that the Fort Hood Shooting had certain elements which were common to both workplace violence and ideologically motivated mass shootings.

Welner believed that Hasan wanted to make a 'spectacle' out of the incident. He further clarified his stance, stating that even a 'trauma care worker' under severe mental distress would not display such homicidal tendencies towards the patients coming in for treatment. According to the forensic psychiatrist, Hasan resorted to taking such an action because of his ideology. Hasan's ideological beliefs came before his Hippocratic Oath, which made him go on a rampage against his colleagues at Fort Hood base. According to Welner, this ideology that took him over was evident by his shout of 'Allahu Akbar' before he opened fire at the scene.

The shooting incident started a debate among scholars and analysts regarding its premise. While many labeled it a terrorist attack, there were others who deemed it as act of violence on account of mental instability. A defense analyst, Carl Tobias, was of the opinion that the incident was not so much of an act of terrorism. He stated that it had more in common with the Virginia Tech massacre that took place when a mentally ill student opened fire on campus. There were many people who believed that, while terrorism could not be ruled out, preliminary evidence suggested that it was not entirely a terrorist attack.

The former United States Attorney General and the retired former head of Bin Laden Issue Station both referred to the incident as a terrorist attack. Terrorism expert, Walid Phares, was also of the opinion that the event was an act of terrorism and Hasan Nidal was a terrorist.

On Anderson Cooper 360 Degrees, General Retired Barrey McCaffrey said that it was beginning to look like the shooting was a 'domestic terrorist attack' on fellow soldiers of the U.S Army by one of their majors who was not loyal to his own men and force.

His former colleagues stated that Hasan's substandard work raised some major concerns, and they found his frequent outbursts expressing extreme Islamic views deeply disturbing. He was also very vocal about his opposition to the wars in Iraq and Afghanistan led by the United States. Hasan's superiors admitted that he seemed mentally unstable and exhibited signs of paranoia. Throughout his tenure at Walter Reed Medical Center, his mental state was discussed a number of times during several office meetings.

An employee of the Center for the Study of Hate and Extremism, Brian Levin, wrote about the Fort Hood shooting and analyzed the motives behind it. According to him, the case was at a 'crossroad' between crime and terrorism incited from mental distress. In his analysis, Levin compared the role that religion played in the events of the day to that of Scott Roeder and his beliefs. Roeder was a devout Christian who was responsible for the murder of Dr. George Tiller who used to perform abortions. Levin wrote that people who commit such acts of terror often 'self-radicalize' as a result of suffering through personal instability, psychological distress and ideological differences. He said that such individuals usually adapt their ideology to justify their anti-social tendencies.

During his trial in 2013, Hasan's motives became clear as he himself admitted to being radicalized and in favor of Islamic extremism. Hasan Nidal explained his motives behind carrying out the shooting at Fort Hood, and those documents made the rounds on all media channels. In those documents, Hasan had frequently used the abbreviation SoA, which allegedly stands for Soldier of Allah. In one of the documents, he wrote about how he was obligated to renounce any kind of oath that would require him to honor a man-made constitutional law over the Islamic commandments.

There was another document in which he expressed his desire to guide and help people in the attainment of heaven. He was quoted as saying, "*I invite the world to read the book of All-Mighty Allah and decide for themselves, if it is the truth from their Lord. My desire is to help people attain heaven by the mercy of their Lord.*"

Hasan was also of the opinion that the differences between the American way of governance and the religion of Islam were too many. He wrote that American democracy and Islamic values could never reconcile; within the American democracy, 'the people' govern according to what they think is right, even if it goes against the will of the 'All-Mighty God'.

Furthermore, he explained that the previous attempts to separate the State from the Church did not do any good for the non-believers. Islam was a better religion than all others, and according to him, it was brought 'to prevail over all' and not be equal or submissive to any other. His statements in the documents were analyzed by scholars who concluded that not only was he a radical Islamist; he had severe mental issues as well.

***

The President of the United States, Barack Obama, made his first official statement regarding the shooting at Fort Hood during his speech at the Tribal Nations Conference. The Conference, held to commemorate the United States' 564 formally recognized Native American tribes, saw President Obama speak about the shooting during his speech. However, the media reaction was unfavorable as many people were of the opinion that the President should have spoken about it at greater length, rather than the three minutes he talked about the shooting.

But the President silenced the critics by arriving at a memorial held for the fallen soldiers in the Fort Hood shooting and delivering a eulogy for all the victims. The reaction to his memorial eulogy was largely positive. A number of journalists even categorized the speech as one of his best ever.

Up until recently, the President had refrained from commenting on the nature of the attack. However, on December 6, 2015, during a speech in which he addressed the fight against terrorism, he included the Fort Hood shooting incident among all the terrorist attacks inspired by Islamic radicalization.

The shootings at Fort Hood were condemned by all the Muslim groups in America. The Council on American-Islamic Relations gave an official statement condemning the shootings and highlighting the fact that the events of the day were not in accordance with the teachings of Islam.

A representative for the Council said that all the Americans should treat the shooting incident as an act committed by a 'deranged individual'. He further clarified that there are some disturbed people among them who could use the religion to further their own cause, and they were not a part of the Muslim community.

The Council member explicitly stated that the community of Muslims condemned the Fort Hood attack.

As for Hasan's relatives and family, they stated that his actions had nothing to do with their family values. One of his cousins said that what Hasan did that day was 'deplorable and despicable'. His relatives went on to say that Hasan might have acted out as a result of severe mental frustration because their religious values did not justify such actions. Their family had not raised their children in such a way, and no one could actually come up with a concrete reason as to what went wrong with Hasan.

As a result of the Fort Hood attack, the Army placed more restrictions on their policy of personal firearms carried onto the bases. Most military weapons that are allowed on bases are used only for security purposes and for training.

Personal weapons that are carried by military officers within the base are usually those which have been registered with the provost marshal and are secured by their owners. A specialist working at the Readiness Center stated that this policy regarding personal firearms had left most of the soldiers on base vulnerable in case of an attack. He said that, while overseas, all military personnel are trained and ready for attack; here they were left exposed and unable to defend themselves. In essence, military bases in the US are gun-free zones, something that I believe is ridiculous.

***

While the investigating officials found no evidence tying Hasan to any extremist terror group or the Al-Qaeda as it was being speculated, they were able to trace some of his e-mails back to Anwar Al-Awlaki. [29]

Just after the attack, Al-Awlaki himself praised Hasan for his actions. In a post on his website, he wrote that Hasan was a hero who had defended Islam. His post also talked about how fighting against the United States was a 'duty' of all the Muslims and nobody could dispute this fact. In his opinion, Hasan had committed an act of heroism by killing all those soldiers who were going to be deployed in Afghanistan and Iraq and were eventually going to kill Muslims there.

In 2010, Al-Awlaki made a statement claiming that the Obama administration was covering up the truth from the public by making the incident look like an act of terror committed by a deranged individual. Within the same year, the authorities were informed that Al-Awlaki was being hunted by the Yemen government and had gone into hiding.

During the end of September 2011, Al-Awlaki and Samir Khan were killed when two Predator drones targeted a vehicle with both of them on board.

***

The criminal investigation against Hasan Nidal was jointly conducted by the FBI, the Texas Rangers Division and the

United States Army Criminal Investigation Command. Hasan was a member of the U.S. Army which subjected him to the jurisdiction of military law (Uniform Code of Military Justice).

Initially, Hasan was being represented by John. P. Gilligan, who was also a retired Army Colonel. He acted as the shooter's defense attorney for some time in the early stages of investigation. On the 9th of November, Hasan regained his consciousness but refused to talk to anybody, including the investigating officials. The officer in charge of investigating and conducting his Article 32 hearing was a U.S Army Colonel, James L. Pohl. Colonel Pohl had previously served on a Guantanamo military commission and had also overseen the investigation against the U.S soldiers charged with the Abu Ghraib abuse.

On the very same day, the officials from FBI investigating the shooting declared that Hasan had acted by himself and did not have any ties with a terrorist organization. Evidence had been reviewed and, while his communication with Anwar Al-Awlaki raised concerns, no such indication of him receiving any orders from anybody had been found.

During a press release issued on November 11, the investigating officials stated that they had carried out a preliminary examination of all his internet activity and work. Emphasis was put on the 'early stages' of the review, and up until now they had not found any information or indication of him being connected to a terrorist network. The speculation that the Fort Hood incident might have been a part of a bigger terror plot was also proved baseless. His communications did not reveal any contact being established with a renowned terror group or any outside facilitator.

The investigating officials researched his background, trying to find any possibility of a meeting between him and Al-Awlaki. They tried to determine whether Hasan was influenced by the Imam's teachings or not, since it had been discovered that Hasan was praying at the same mosque where Al-Awlaki had mentored the 9/11 hijackers. Army officials who were working on the case stated that research was ongoing and they were yet to find any concrete evidence.

Army officials made a statement saying that they were operating under the belief that Hasan had most likely acted alone. They refrained from commenting on the motives behind the shooting until further investigation. Furthermore, it was believed that Hasan had recently written a post on the Internet, expressing his support for suicide bombings.

Despite the regular updates issued by the investigators and Army officials regarding the case, rumors and speculation continued to surround the cause of the shooting. Senator Leiberman made a statement addressing the issue and even shared his own opinion on it: Hasan was suffering from severe mental stress and might have turned towards extremist Islamism to relieve his frustration.

After the investigation had been completed, the Department of Justice came to an agreement on Hasan's trial. It was decided that he would be tried in military court. Many scholars and analysts observed that this decision was consistent with the investigators' conclusion that Hasan had been acting alone and had no help from anyone.

On November 21, a hearing in Hasan's hospital room took place, where a magistrate ruled that there was 'probable cause' that he was the shooter who had opened fire within the Fort Hood Army base. The judge also ordered that, because of the probable cause, Hasan should be held in pretrial confinement when released by the hospital doctors.

He was charged and convicted on thirteen counts of premeditated murder and thirty-two counts of attempted murder. The charges of attempted murder were made by the Army officials who had investigated the shooting. Apart from those, there were additional charges against Hasan pending a court martial.

The prosecutors, who had charged Hasan on the thirteen murder counts, did not include the death of the fetus that Francheska Velez was carrying. Such charges can be made by the prosecutors under the Unborn Victims of Violence Act, as well as *Article 119a* of the Uniform Code of Military Justice.

Hasan's case raised quite a debate among scholars, politicians and the public, too. If the civilian prosecutors on his case had indicted him for terrorism or having any sort of association with a terrorist network, his case could have been tried at the federal criminal level that comes under the U.S. Anti-Terrorism laws. The military justice system had not prosecuted a death penalty case since 1961, and rarely have people been sentenced since then. Hence, his trial and sentencing created quite a furor, as it was something quite unprecedented on the part of the military justice system.

***

On July 20, 2011, Hasan was formally arraigned, but he did not enter a plea. However, the judge granted his attorney's request that a formal plea would be entered at a later date. This date was not specified by the attorneys or the judge.

Initially, the trial date for Hasan's court martial was set by the judge as March 5th, 2012. This was pushed back to later when Hasan changed lawyers and more time had to be allotted to them to prepare a defense in his case. The judge, Colonel

Gregory Gross, instructed Hasan to follow Army protocol and have his beard shaved when he showed up in court. Hasan did not adhere to the instructions and was found in contempt of court after he turned up without shaving his beard. Judge Gross fined him for this in July 2012.

Finally his court martial date was decided to be August 20th, 2012, and his trial was to begin. Hasan showed up again without shaving his beard and was fined yet another time for still keeping his beard. He was warned that his beard could be shaved forcibly before his court martial began.

By the 15th of August, Hasan was to enter his pleas against the charges that had been made against him before the court martial was set. The prosecution was pursuing a death penalty against the charges of premeditated murder, which meant that Hasan would not be allowed to enter a guilty plea. At that time, Hasan's only objection was to being forcibly shaved as he maintained that having a beard was a part of his religious beliefs. His attorneys appealed to the United States Court of Appeals for the Armed Forces and asked for an exemption to the rule. They argued that

Hasan should not have to shave his beard against his will.

On the 27th of August, the Appeals court ruled that the trial should be allowed to continue as this was no reason for it to be halted. They did not specify whether he should be made to shave his beard or permitted to retain it. Previously, the United States Court of Appeals for Armed Forces had rejected Hasan's attempts to obtain an exemption from Army regulations and be 'religiously accommodated' as far as his appearance was concerned.

A week later, it was determined that the Religious Freedom Restoration Act (1993) was not relevant in this case, which led to Judge Gross ruling that Hasan should indeed be shaved according to Army regulations. However, the order could not be implemented until all of his appeals were exhausted. This meant that the trial could experience further delays.

When the hearing took place on the 6th of September, 2012, Hasan offered to plead guilty on both counts. However, at the time, the Army regulations could not allow the judge to accept a guilty plea in a death penalty case. On September 21st, Hasan Nidal's attorneys filed two more appeals in the Army Court of Criminal Appeals against the shaved beard order. This delayed the trial even further, giving rise to feelings of dissension among the residents of Killeen. People were clearly not happy about the delays.

During October, the Court of Appeals upheld Judge Gross's order of forcibly shaving Hasan's beard off. In response to that, Hasan's lawyers filed an appeal in the Court of Appeals for the Armed Forces, asking for the removal of Judge Gross from the case and the overturning of the lower court.

On the 4th of December, 2012, the Court of Appeals for the Armed Forces ruled in favor of the appeal, removing Judge Gross from the case, citing requisite impartiality as a reason behind their decision. The court also vacated Major Hasan's six convictions for contempt of court. The Court of Appeals also overturned the order for forcible shaving of Hasan's beard. However, the violation of his religious rights was not addressed.

Furthermore, the ruling stated that Hasan could keep his beard for the time being, as his appearance in court was the military command's responsibility and not the concern of a military judge.

The Army Judge Advocate General was able to appoint a replacement for Judge Gross in time and get the trial started.

The ruling by the Court of Appeals was referred to as rare and unusual, with many scholars saying that something like that had never happened in this kind of a case.

Colonel Tara A. Osborn was appointed in place of Colonel Gross on the very same day and assumed her responsibility as the Judge on the case. The trial was scheduled to continue in 2013. Judge Osborn had to make a few important decisions before it could officially begin. Hasan's defense attorney claimed that LTG Campbell had not been completely impartial when he ruled for the death penalty, which led to Judge Osborn deliberating upon its removal from the case. However, on the 31st of January,

2013, Judge Osborn ruled in favor of a capital trial and deemed it constitutional, citing a Supreme Court Case of 1996 involving Dwight J. Loving.

Osborn also ruled that the court did not have any jurisdiction regarding his appearance or beard, and that matter had to be dealt with his military chain of command.

In February 2013, Hasan's court martial date was set as May 29th, 2013, with jury selection being held through July.

On the 3rd of June, 2013, a military judge allowed Hasan to represent himself in his murder trial that was about to begin. His attorneys were to stay on the case but on the sidelines, and they were only to come in for help if required. The jury selection process took place during the summer, after which the trial was to officially begin. On the 6th of August, 2013, opening statements were presented in the court. Judge Osborn had already ruled beforehand that Hasan could not claim defense of Taliban as a reason for his actions.

The trial began on August 6th, 2013,

after the opening statements had been recorded. During this time, Hasan interacted with the American media for the first time. In an interview, he stated that the shooting at Fort Hood had been his way of acting out against the United States. He claimed that the United States military was at war with Islam, and his actions were justified since he was defending his religion.

During the first day of his trial, Hasan confessed to being the shooter at Fort Hood and also stated that the authorities would find evidence supporting his confession. He outright admitted to being the gunman who had opened fire at the Fort Hood Army base in 2009. He told the military panel that he had 'switched sides' and considered himself as a 'mujahideen' carrying out 'Jihad' against the enemy of Islam. His defense strategy led to disagreements between him and his lawyers who were trying to get the death penalty sentence removed. Since Hasan was representing himself, his lawyers did not have much say in the proceedings; however, they disagreed upon his defense statements. According to them, Hasan's defense strategy was working in the favor of a death penalty instead of obtaining its removal.

On the 23rd of August, 2013, Hasan was convicted on account of all the charges made against him. The jury reached the conviction after deliberating for seven hours. Just five days after that conviction, a military court ruled in favor of a death penalty. He was sentenced to death for shooting and killing thirteen people and injuring more than thirty.

He became the sixth person to be put on a military death row.

Influence of ISIS

The terror group known as the Islamic State of Iraq and the Levant has been on the rise since 2014. In a couple of years, it has expanded rapidly and has made its presence felt throughout the globe. Previously its terror activities were restricted to the Middle East; however, in the last year, they have been expanded to the European and American regions as well.

It all began in Iraq with the establishment of the network in 2004. Allegedly the Islamists had formed the group to drive the American troops out of their country. The founding leader of the group was notorious terrorist Abu Musab Al-Zarqawi.

After Al-Zarqawi was shot dead during an American raid in 2006, Abu Abdullah al-Rashid al-Baghdadi became the 'Emir' of the group, renaming Islamic State and making it their mission to turn

Iraq into an Islamic country. However, in 2010, he was shot dead during a joint raid made by the American and Iraqi troops.

The organization conducted an election after the death of their leader, and eventually Abu Bakr al-Baghdadi was chosen as the new leader. He established his authority as a 'Caliph', as he believed that he was one of the descendants of the Prophet Muhammad and this was his right. The Islamic State, under his command, started to expand and increase their terrorist activities.

They not only attacked the American troops, but also the Iraqi soldiers and members of the Shi'ite Mahdi Army. The members of the terrorist group also made it their mission to have the Iraqi government thrown over, as it was their belief that the Iraqi leaders were American 'puppets'. There were several planned bombings in Sunni mosques where the members of ISIS left deliberate evidence implicating the Shi'ite. In this way, they would be able to incite sectarian violence and give rise to the conflict between the Shi'ites and Sunni Muslims.

When the United States called its troops back in 2011, the military pressure on the terrorist organization was eased a little.

In 2013, when the Syrian civil war had begun, the Islamic State began to infiltrate Syria. They fought against the forces of the Syrian leader and claimed that they were doing 'Jihad'. Al-Baghdadi officially named the organization Islamic State of Iraq and Levant, or as it is known in Arabic, the Islamic State of Iraq and al-Sham.

This served as an official expansion for the group as it was no longer confined within the Iraqi borders. It had managed to mark its presence in Syria and was openly promoting the 'Jihad. Sometime after its establishment in Syria, the terror group struck a major blow to the Syrian Army as well as the secular anti-government forces. They began occupying some of the northern and northeastern parts of Syria. The members of the group marched on ahead, turning the already war-torn areas into a battlefield.

In January 2014, the ISIS launched

two major offenses in Raqqa and Deir Ezzor. They managed to successfully take over and establish a base within Syria. The leader, Al-Baghdadi, called upon his forces and asked them to connect Iraqi and Syrian groups with each other.

His people marched towards Iraq and captured the cities of Mosul, Fallujah and Tikrit. They also went towards some of the areas in the provinces of Nineveh and Salahuddin. Apart from that, they managed to establish a hold on the crossings at the Iraq-Jordan and Iraq-Syrian borders.

Baghdadi made a formal announcement declaring himself Islamic Caliphate over the areas controlled by the terror group. Its known presence is within almost all the Middle Eastern countries as well as some European regions towards Italy and Spain. The organization, allegedly, has some influence in China's Xinjiang province as well. The leader of the group calls himself the Caliph of all the Muslims and has asked them to join the fight for the establishment of an Islamic capital.

The organization is said to be more cruel and ruthless than the other terrorist groups. Its brutal beheadings and horror treatment of prisoners that they take as 'slaves' has made headlines throughout the globe.

From 2004 to 2014, the terrorists' activities were restricted within Iraqi borders; however, when they infiltrated Syria in 2014, the influence spilled over there as well. More than half of the terrorist attacks in Syria were said to be carried out by the Islamic State.

In June 2014, the ISIS members managed to capture about seventeen hundred soldiers from the province of Nineveh. All of them were brutally and ruthlessly executed. In July, the ISIS executed two-hundred-and-seventy soldiers after gaining a hold of the fields in Central Syria.

During the end of July 2014, the organization posted a number of videos in which they showed how they were destroying Shi'ite mosques and killing the Shi'ite Muslims. In August, they went on an 'ethnic' cleansing spree and started targeting the Yezidis living in the Sinjar region of Iraq. The members of the organization began killing all the men who refused to convert to the religion of Islam. The Yezidi women and girls were taken as sex 'slaves'.

It has been noted that up to fifty thousand Yezidis have made the journey to the mountains, leaving their homes behind. Many have also sought shelter in the refugee camps established in the northern region of Iraq.

The ISIS also posted videos in August and September, respectively, showing the beheading of two American journalists, James Foley and Steven Sotloff.

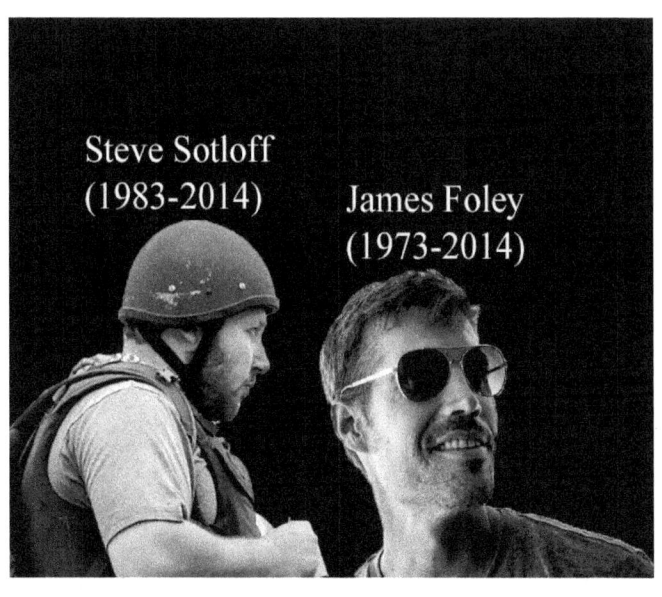

213

It's interesting to mention that the parents of both journalists were warned not to pay any ransom to the Jihadi terrorists or face federal charges.

Since 2014, it is believed that the ISIS has increased its militant forces from ten thousand to over ninety thousand. They are divided between Iraq and Syria. They control an area of 260,000 square kilometers, with Iraqi and Chechen militants spread all over the Iraqi and Syrian regions.

The organization started to expand its influence by recruiting members from all over the world, especially third or fourth generation Muslims living in Europe and America. It is said that their forces also include a number of Caucasians who converted to Islam and went on to join the organization.

Apart from that, the group has even invited a number of government leaders to join their cause, especially those from the Saddam Hussein regime.

There has been much speculation regarding the source of funding for the group. While many have accused the Saudi

Arabian government of funding them, nothing has been proven so far. The Saudis deny having any involvement with the ISIS. Analysts say that the Saudis and other Arab groups could not possibly fund the terrorist organizations. They are of the opinion that ISIS thrives on the spoils of war.

Every time they have conquered an area, they have established a hold on its resources. The members of the groups rob banks, steal jewelry and sell any historical artifacts they come across. They are also known for destroying ancient relics instead of selling them. Recently, the ancient city of Palmyra made headlines when it was threatened by the ISIS forces. The city had been termed as a 'world heritage site' by UNESCO and has reportedly been suffering from threats of destruction as the ISIS wages war on it.

The ISIS levies taxes on people in the areas they control and then publicly executes those who don't pay them. They have also set up checkpoints to collect taxes from any vehicles that want to pass by any of the areas under their rule. It has also been observed that the ISIS took over gas and oil fields in Iraq and Syria. According to some analysts, they might even be selling gas and oil to some of the countries.

The intelligence agencies in Iraq estimate the group has funds of over two billion dollars, out of which $430 million is in cash while the rest is in the form of gold bars. The ISIS forces have also taken over a vast amount of military arsenal in both Syria and Iraq. Many are of the opinion that the ISIS forces have military grade equipment and weaponry that is far more powerful than that of Al-Qaeda, Hezbollah and other terrorist factions combined. It was noted that when the ISIS raided the Syrian Tabqa air base and an airport in Mosul, they managed to get a hold of a dozen 'Black Hawk 'helicopters and MiG-23 fighter jets.

As the influence of ISIS has risen, it has also attracted the attention of other terrorist groups. Some of them pledge their allegiance to it, while the others just try to follow their strategies. In November 2013, the head of a huge Chechen militant group expressed his support for ISIS and pledged allegiance to them. When the group became the Islamic State, the leader of the Chechen militant group stated that Chechnya was also a part of the Islamic Caliphate.

In July 2014, the leader of the Nigerian terrorist group, Boko Haram, announced the integration of his group within the ISIS network. He also said that Nigeria, Cameroon, Chad and Niger will be a part of the Islamic Caliphate. In the same year, a terrorist faction from South Asia also pledged its allegiance with the organization, expressing that South Asia will also become an important part of the Islamic Caliphate.

The Al-Qaeda factions across the Arabian Peninsula and other regions of Afghanistan support the network but have not pledged their allegiance to it. There are some who oppose its activities and claim that there is a difference of ideologies between them and ISIS.

***

The spillover effects of ISIS have not only impacted the countries in the Middle East but other nations across Asia, Africa and even Europe as well. The ISIS considers all the nations who are allied with the United States as enemies of Islam, and its mission is to wage 'Jihad' against them all.

The terrorist activities of the network have expanded across a number of countries which in turn have seen a rise in terrorism since 2014. Taliban factions in Pakistan, the Al-Qaeda in Afghanistan, Islamic movements in South East Asia, and other terror groups across the Middle East have all admitted to being inspired by their activities. This has led these terrorist factions to launch offensives in their regions.

There have been frequent terrorist attacks in Pakistan, with the most destructive being the attack on an Army school in Peshawar, which left over a hundred-and-forty students dead. The Pakistani Taliban has also claimed responsibility for causing many other disruptions in government protests or against the Pakistan Army.

In Nigeria, Boko Haram has been on a continuous offensive, leading to the displacement of over sixty-five-thousand people. The security situation in the countries of Lebanon, Yemen and Somalia is also fast deteriorating.

The past year saw the spillover effect proceed to the European region. The Charlie Hebdo attacks and then the Paris Attack in November established the fact that the ISIS's influence has crossed over. A lot of people lost their lives with many suffering traumatic injuries and permanent wounds. The Charlie Hebdo attacks left about eleven people dead when two terrorists made their way into the offices of Charlie Hebdo, a satirical newspaper in Paris. They opened fire on the people at the office, killing eleven and injuring many others in the building.

Among the dead was a member of the French National Police, who was shot when the terrorists made their way out of the building.

The Paris attacks were a series of coordinated attacks that occurred in different locations throughout Paris and left 130 people dead. Around 368 people were injured. The attacks occurred throughout a restaurant, Bataclan Theatre where a concert was going on, and a couple of other places in Paris. The terrorists killed around eighty-nine people at Bataclan Theatre after a standoff with the police which involved them taking a number of people hostages before killing them.

During the attacks, the terrorists opened fire on a number of people, while a couple of them set off bombs. Later investigation revealed that the terrorists had suicide vests strapped on as well.

The attacks led to strong offensive being launched by the countries of France, Russia and United Kingdom against the ISIS. The ISIS territories in Syria and Iraq were targeted by missiles and fighter drones which bombarded the areas.

This also led to global attention being drawn to the plague that is the ISIS, with many countries increasing their efforts to thwart the terrorist activities of the organization.

***

The influence of ISIS has been on the rise and there is no denying it. With each day, there is news coming in of people across the globe leaving their home countries and fleeing to Syria to join the organization. Self-radicalization has been one factor that has seen a number of young boys and girls going off to join the ISIS in their 'Jihad' against the enemies of Islam.

Analysts believe that its movements have been most successful in Australia, United Kingdom and Asia.

It has been believed that about a hundred-and-twenty Australians are among the ISIS militants. They joined the movement and are now fighting the war in Iraq and Syria. There are others who have answered its call to 'Jihad' by planning terrorist attacks in their own areas and are inspired by the group.

The government has taken strict actions to prevent its people from being recruited by the organization. Bans have been placed on traveling to certain areas in Iraq and Syria, while passports of people believed to be involved in any way in criminal activities are being canceled.

Perhaps the most success the organization has had with recruitment is within the United Kingdom. Young girls and boys, mostly Muslim immigrants and even converts, have gone off to join the ISIS movement in Syria and Iraq. Young girls have quit school and left their families to go to Syria and become 'jihadi brides'.

There have been reports of hassled parents in a number of countries across Europe looking for their children who go missing. Later, it turns out that many of them left and went to Syria through Turkey to join the ISIS. Governments have acted quickly on this matter, taking action against the people who travel to Turkey and then move onward to Syria from there.

Turkey has actually been integral to this movement. Many recruits that want to join the organization first arrive in Turkey and then go off to Syria. Turkish authorities have tried to curb this and have introduced stricter checks on their airports and borders. Other than that, Turkey also has suffered from a rising ISIS influence with the country. Some of the worst terrorist attacks in the history of the country were carried out in the past year in Ankara, the capital, and other cities as well.

In the Asian regions, the ISIS has also strengthened. In countries like Bangladesh and Pakistan, terrorism has been on the rise. Continuous turmoil and a volatile situation have actually provided a fertile breeding ground for terrorist factions. A number of terrorist activities in these regions have been linked to ISIS. Even India suffers from the threat of increasing radicalism, with many Indian Muslims looking to follow radical Islam.

For many years, South East Asia has had a fairly smooth and peaceful conduct as far as faith is concerned. The Muslims in the region have practiced their religion in harmony and have had little tolerance for radicalism. However, it looks like the situation might experience some turmoil. The Islamic movements in the region have expressed their support for the ISIS and seem to be taking to their strategies of terror.

According to some figures, around six hundred Indonesians have joined the ISIS as yet. In March, the Indonesian elite force detained five people who were accused of facilitating a dozen people in custody of Turkish authorities for violations of travel laws. These people were known to be traveling to Syria from Turkey and had been stopped at a checkpoint and taken into custody for questioning.

The Indonesian authorities are also leading a joint investigation with Turkish police and searching for a group of sixteen people that went missing in Istanbul.

Further evidence of the ISIS gaining a stronghold in the region is the attack in Jakarta, just weeks into January 2016. The attack within the Indonesian capital saw four civilians and four terrorists being killed. A Starbucks was bombed after which a shootout with the police followed at a traffic police post. Indonesian police were able to arrest thirteen suspects after the incident and even killed one of them.

Militancy in the region has always been in check. However, it has always had a presence. It looks like the ISIS might be capitalizing on that in order to further their movement. The region has a number of hidden areas outside state control which the militants can use to establish their base. In fact, some of the islands of Philippines and Malaysia have been home to long running insurgencies from the Muslim minorities as well.

In these regions, like Malaysia and Philippines, the government has had a firm control on outside actors. However, in recent times, even these countries have seen a rise in radicalism and the threat of terrorism. Recently, the Malaysian police arrested a man at a bar who was threatening to blow himself up. Three other Malaysians were arrested by Turkish authorities and deported back to the country after being caught trying to cross over to Syria. According to some figures, about a hundred Malaysians have gone off and joined the ISIS.

Malaysian authorities stated that they were doing everything they could to curb those figures and introduced new travel laws involving the revoking or suspension of documents of anyone believed to be involved in a terrorist activity. The situation in the Philippines is similar. Unconfirmed figures report that a hundred young Muslim Filipinos have gone on to join the 'Jihadist' group, while the government and authorities state that they have not found any such links between terrorist factions in the region and ISIS. The officials in the Philippines also say that the government is on the lookout and ready to take immediate action against anyone found to be involved in such an activity or group.

Singaporean authorities stated that in the previous year they had arrested twenty-seven Bangladeshis plotting a terrorist attack within their city and were repatriating them to their own country.

One very surprising development has been in the island of Maldives. The place is known for its scenic beauty and luxury resorts, and terrorism is the last thing that one would associate with such a place. Some analysts and journalists say that the place has turned into one of the biggest recruiting grounds for ISIS. Media reports have stated that a number of ISIS members killed in action come from the little island of Maldives.

While the authorities have refrained from commenting on such reports, there has been speculation that the government might be introducing some new travel laws.

Other than that, the ISIS presence in Central Asia has also raised some questions. According to analysts, the number of people who have joined the movement range from three hundred to somewhere near five hundred. It is also being said that the organization might have established ties with the Xinjiang province in China.

With the spread of the ISIS, many countries have been threatened by trans-national terrorism. It could have a serious impact on the political stability and economic situation of a country. Taking the example of Singapore, one can see why it takes its security so seriously. The small country of Singapore is sandwiched between Malaysia and Indonesia, both of which are predominantly Muslim countries.

Singapore, on the other hand, has a multiracial society and culture which could be affected very negatively if the situation in any of its neighboring countries became volatile. The spillover effect would definitely spread over to the small country of Singapore.

***

Just a year before, ISIS became IS with Al-Baghdadi proclaiming that the Islamic State was for all. The movement of the organization took on a more global scale with the militants declaring widespread war.

The IS, Islamic State, involved itself with a bigger agenda that would lead to them becoming a recognized Caliphate. With that rose the 'jihadist' phenomenon that caused a number of countries to take immediate and strict action against the organization.

The United States was already involved in a military air action against the IS, with their drones and jets carrying out regular air strikes on their bases in Iraq. Soon Russia, the United Kingdom and France also joined in the offensive against it.

While many sources agree that the influence of IS might be receding, there is still a long way to go until it is completely eliminated.

The recent year has seen the migrant crisis spiral out of control with thousands migrating to Europe from the war-torn regions of Syria. Most of the migrants that are making the journey have been driven out by the fear of IS militants killing them and their families.

Most of the stories reported by these migrants are tales of horror and brutality. The IS militants bomb houses, abduct children and torture the families, causing them to leave everything behind and flee.

The United Nations have shed light on the issue of the Yezidi girls who are taken by the IS as sex slaves. These are young girls who are raped and tortured by the militants in an attempt to forcibly convert them to Islam. The UN has called for an increase in efforts to try and rehabilitate the girls who have escaped the militants and fled to refugee camps.

Despite all the efforts to thwart the influence of the Islamic State, the radical Islamist thought still prevails. The IS has continued to capitalize on that and move ahead. According to some officials, around fifteen hundred Britons have joined the terrorist organization thus far. The organization has also been responsible for destroying historical sites and relics and burning down some of the oldest libraries as well.

Since its rise, the IS has made headlines for its brutality. It has carried out mass executions, public beheadings and numerous other cruel acts. The organization has a presence within the social media and has posted videos showing their acts of brutality for everyone to see.

The media has time and again emphasized the need for extensive action against the organization. Many scholars and officials have also spoken out against their terrorist activities and brutal acts in the name of Islam. Many Islamic scholars have come forward and stated that the organization has nothing to do with Islam. They cite incidents from Islamic history and verses from the Koran which preach tolerance and call for a peaceful co-existence.

However, the IS has remained firm in their belief that whatever they are doing is for the cause of Islam. They are of the opinion that Muslims cannot peacefully co-exist with the non-believers. Their movement is a 'Jihad' against the non-believers and an attempt to establish the authority of Islam all over the world.

The countries of the world have made a united stand against the IS, and there is hope that, in the time to come, the organization will be finished. A number of countries have called for action and even introduced new laws to curb terrorism, so it seems likely that the recruitment program being run by the organization will be put to a stop.

There is still much to be done to eradicate the influence of IS completely; however, in the light of recent developments, it might look like a possibility in the near future.

Self-Radicalization Recruiting through Social Media

The terrorist attacks that have occurred throughout the world post-9/11 are innumerable. With the rise of ISIS and other terrorist factions, things seem to have taken a turn for the worse in the past few years. This rise in terrorism can be attributed to the rapid spread of radicalization throughout the decade.

Radicalization has been an ever present phenomenon in history, particularly when it comes to religion. Religious radicalization is something that has been a matter of concern for governments and agencies across the globe. While it was always a persistent problem through time, it was never such a prominent widespread issue as it is today. After the 9/11 attacks, religious radicalization primarily became Islamic radicalization, and terrorism became associated with Al-Qaeda.

Islamic radicalization has spread rapidly in the past decade or so, becoming a major global security issue. The emergence and rise of social media, easy communication and advancement in technology have all aided this spread of Islamic radicalization. In fact, it has been able to reach as far and wide as it has because of these factors. The internet and social media, in particular, provided Islamist radicals with a platform that enabled them to target an audience in any country of the world.

Islamist radicals are using different social networks and media channels to get their message across to different people across the globe. It is how self-radicalization has occurred.

The term self-radicalization is used to describe the acts of terrorism committed by individual terrorists that are not associated with any organization but are just inspired by their ideology. It has become quite popular in the recent years, especially since the rise of ISIS.

In the past five years or so, there has been a significant increase in the terrorist activities carried out by these self-radicalized, 'lone-wolf' terrorists who are not directly a part of any terrorist organization. Looking back at the terrorist incidents from the last three to five years, one can see that the attacks launched by these self-radicalized terrorists are more than the mass murders carried out by terrorist organizations.

Self-radicalization has been closely associated with social media, with many even saying that the social networks and internet regulations are to be blamed for its rise. This is not entirely the case. While the internet and social networking have definitely made it easier, it is not the only reason why there is an increase in the self-radicalized lone-wolf terrorist. There are many factors that come into play: personal lives, mental condition, environment, government policies, and many such things that can cause a person to resort to terrorism.

However, most of the time, these self-radicalized terrorists are just extremists trying to impose their ideology on others through violence. These self-radicalized individuals have actually attacked a number of places, wreaking havoc and murdering many innocent civilians in their path. In 2002, there was the Washington, D.C. Sniper attacks that killed over a dozen people, then in 2009 the Fort Hood shooting occurred, and more recently there were two shooting incidents in Canada during 2014 that killed and wounded soldiers. The most destructive of these attacks occurred in 2015 in San Bernardino, claiming the lives of fourteen people and injuring twenty-two.

Washington, D.C. Sniper Attacks

The Washington, D.C. sniper attacks that took place in October 2002 were a series of coordinated shootings occurring over a course of three weeks. The shootings were carried out at random in Maryland, Virginia and Washington, D.C., killing ten people and gravely injuring three.

The victims were targeted at random over different locations across the metropolitan area in Washington, D.C. and Interstate 95 in Virginia. These attacks brought life in these areas to a virtual standstill, creating panic and fear in people all over the country. The perpetrators of the attacks were John Allen Muhammad, aged forty-two, and Lee Boyd Malvo, who at that time was only seventeen years old. [30]

On October 2, 2002, the attack was launched as a bullet shattered through a window in a craft store located in Aspen Hill, Maryland. The shot narrowly missed the cashier, Ann Chapman, and nobody was injured. This shooting did not raise much alarm in the area at the time. However, just an hour later, James Martin, a fifty-five-year-old man was shot and killed in the parking lot of a grocery store in Wheaton, Maryland.

John Allen Muhammad, 42, and Lee Boyd Malvo, 17

Initially, the police did not find enough evidence linking the two incidents; however, they soon realized that this was just the beginning of a chain of shootings that would spread across Washington and other areas in Virginia and Maryland.

On the morning of October 3, 2002, four people were shot and killed within a time period of two hours across Aspen Hill and Montgomery County. There was a fifth victim shot in the evening of the same day in the District of Columbia, near Silver Spring, Maryland. All of the victims were randomly targeted, not of any particular race, gender, age, caste or creed. In each of the shootings, the shooters had fired a single shot from a distance and then disappeared.

This particular pattern was discovered after the day when all five victims were found dead in various places.

As the news about the shooting spread through the region, the fear and panic among the public began to rise. Schools were put on a code blue alert, with children being locked indoors until the place was declared secure. Private schools went on lockdown, as did other areas where there could be a danger of shooting. Parents went to pick up their children early and kept them indoors throughout the day, not allowing them to go to public places or out on the road alone.

Soon the police were able to determine that all of the bullets fired were from the same gun and the shootings were connected. The reports at the beginning were conflicting; some people said that they had seen a white box truck near the Silver Spring area, while others were reporting differently. After the murder in Washington, D.C., witnesses told the police officials that there was no white box truck, instead it was a blue Chevrolet Caprice. The police were unable to find any clear leads as yet.

From then onward, the shooters started putting a gap of two to three days in between each shooting. In the course of twenty days, six more victims were shot, out of which one thirteen-year-old boy was the only survivor. When the police found the boy and took him to the hospital, they also found a Tarot card that bore the inscription 'Call Me God'. Later it was submitted as evidence in Muhammad's trial.

On October 22, 2002, Conrad Johnson, a bus driver, was confirmed as the tenth fatality when he was shot on the steps of his bus.

***

The investigation was headed by the FBI, the United States Secret Service, and involved the Montgomery Police Chief,

Charles Moose, as well as other police departments who investigated in their areas of jurisdiction. Progress in investigation was slow as the numerous reports were coming in from various places and most of them were confused and unclear.

Police officials kept on receiving tips and information from the hotline they had set up. All the while, the teams worked on putting together all of the evidence and finding links to anybody that could give them an indication of the shooter.

The investigators made headway when the shooters themselves tried to engage the police in dialogue. One of the phone calls was traced to a payphone in Henrico County, Virginia, but the suspects narrowly missed the police. Police officials also found other notes and Tarot cards with threatening messages and demands for money written on them.

Soon enough, the shooters called out to the police again. This time it was through a priest in Ashland, Virginia. The shooters told him to ask the police about an unsolved robbery-homicide shooting that occurred in a liquor store in Montgomery,

Alabama, on September 21, 2002. Evidence found on the scene had fingerprints which were matched to those that had been discovered by the police during one of the shootings.

Investigating officers discovered that the fingerprints belonged to Lee Boyd Malvo, a seventeen-year-old boy from Jamaica. His fingerprints had been in the system since 2001 when he had been registered by the United States Immigration and Naturalization Service. It was soon determined that Malvo had ties with John Allen Muhammad and had been seen traveling with him. Muhammad was a Persian Gulf War Veteran and an expert marksman.

Police found Muhammad's ex-wife living in Maryland and were informed about an automobile that he had recently purchased in New Jersey.

The information about the automobile helped the police obtain the license plate number of the blue Chevrolet Caprice which belonged to Muhammad. A warrant for federal arms violations was issued in his name and a description of the vehicle was sent out to all police radios and media channels.

***

Twenty-two days after the first shooting incident, the perpetrators were arrested. On October 24, 2002, both Muhammad and Malvo were found sleeping in the Chevrolet Caprice and were apprehended off Interstate 70 in Myersville, Maryland.

Whitey Donohue spotted the car at a rest stop off the Interstate and informed the police. Wayne Smith, Trooper First Class D, belonging to the Maryland State Police, was the first officer to arrive on scene. His quick thinking helped capture the shooters as he blocked off the exit by parking his police car between the two tractor trailers parked around the Chevrolet and sealed the exit way.

Within minutes, more troopers arrived and began to block off every one of the exit and entrance ramps surrounding the area. The suspects at the time were still not aware of the police presence around them.

One of the truck drivers, Ron Lanz, began to move his truck out and exit. He was stopped by the troopers who used his truck to seal off the one remaining exit and round off the road block. As every escape route was now covered, the SWAT team was sent in to arrest the suspects. Both Muhammad and Malvo were taken into custody within minutes.

The police then did a thorough search of the car and found a Bushmaster . 223-caliber assault rifle. It was later concluded that the weapon had been used in eleven of the fourteen shootings. They also found some modifications made to the vehicle, including a concealed firing port in the car's trunk. These modifications enabled the shooter to fire from within the vehicle and go undetected.

***

Initially the investigators were of the opinion that Muhammad was trying to get revenge on his ex-wife, Mildred, who had taken out an order against him and prevented the children from seeing him. However, the Judge ruled that claim as alleged until conclusive evidence regarding the theory was presented in court.

While they were in jail, both Muhammad and Malvo wrote about 'Jihad' against the U.S. Malvo made a number of drawings that exhibited his extremist views and violent tendencies.

In one of the murder trials, a court in Virginia found Muhammad guilty of actions 'pursuant to the direction or order' towards terrorism.

Later on, in 2006, Malvo testified in Muhammad's trial and confessed that they were on a mission to kidnap children and ransom them for money from the government in order to fund their terrorist operations. He claimed that they had wanted to 'set up camp' to train kids on terrorizing cities, and the ultimate goal was to 'shut down' everything within the United States.

***

The proceedings took place in Virginia and Maryland. Muhammad was found guilty on murder charges and received the death penalty. His execution date was set as November 10, 2009.

Malvo was also found guilty on six counts of murder and on June 1, 2006, was sentenced to six life terms without the possibility of parole.

He also testified in Muhammad's trial and gave details on their plans. It turned out that the two of them formulated a multi-phase plan that consisted of three phases. It was to be carried out in Washington and Baltimore and involved a number of other shootings and bomb attacks.

Malvo admitted that the plan did not go off as planned and they had to do something else when phase one and two failed.

The memorial for the Washington, D.C., sniper victims is located in Wheaton, Maryland, with an additional one being built at the government plaza of Rockville.

SNIPER SHOOTING VICTIMS

Bridges · Buchanan · Charlot · Franklin · Lewis-Rivera

Martin · Meyers · Ramos · Walekar · Johnson

Victims of the DC Sniper

Saint-Jean-sur-Richelieu Attack, Canada

This attack was a terror car ramming in Quebec, Canada, that occurred on October 20, 2014. A lone wolf terrorist, Martin Couture-Rouleau, hit two members of the Canadian forces, killing one and severely injuring the other. [31]

At 11:30 a.m., October 20, 2014, Martin Couture-Rouleau rammed a vehicle deliberately into two members of the Canadian Armed Forces. The soldiers happened to be walking across a parking lot in Saint-Jean-sur-Richelieu, Quebec, when they were hit by the vehicle. Couture-Rouleau had been sitting in his car since two hours before carrying out the attacks and was watching the area for possible targets.

He was chased by the police until he rolled his car into a ditch and lost control of it. The car landed on its roof, with a witness stating that a spiked belt had been deployed afterwards. According to some of the bystanders, the driver, Couture-Rouleau stepped out of the vehicle and charged at a female police officer with a knife. The witnesses saw the knife on the ground later after he was taken to the hospital.

Martin Couture-Rouleau

The police officers shot at him about seven times when he launched the attack at the officer and had him on the ground within a few minutes. He was transported to the hospital where he was pronounced dead that evening.

His victims were two officers, one was in uniform at the time he was shot and the other was not. Patrick Vincent, aged fifty-three, died the following day due to injuries while the other survived. The second unnamed soldier sustained wounds that were non-life threatening and was able to pull through.

Patrick Vincent [32] was a Warrant Officer who had served in the military for twenty-eight years. It turned out that he had been considering retirement after serving as an engineer and a firefighter in the military. He had been on the refrigeration and mechanical technician engineer post before going on to military firefighting.

***

Couture-Rouleau was a francophone Canadian who had been living in Saint-Jean-sur-Richelieu when he decided to carry out the attack. He was twenty-five years of age and lived with his parents after being separated from his partner and their infant. He had recently converted to Islam and was seen praying regularly at a mosque.

He owned a washing business that had failed and was unemployed at the time of the attack.

The attack was characterized as a terrorist one by both the RCMP (Royal Canadian Mounted Police) and the government of Canada, including a statement by the Prime Minister, Stephen Harper.

Legal papers were evidence of the fact that Couture-Rouleau had converted to Islam in 2013 and had changed his name to Ahmed LeConverte, which means Ahmed the Converted. Upon investigation, it was revealed that his internet and Facebook activity showed that he had been influenced by the extremist ideology of ISIS and had been supporting them.

He had been posting video links and images that promoted anti-American sentiment and foreign policy. Some of his video links were of anti-Semitic content as well, along with other material that was indication of his rising extremism. Among all that was the interview in which he expressed his support for ISIS.

Other than that, there were reports that he had seen images and posters on Facebook that referenced Islam's superiority over other religions, especially Christianity. One of his friends reportedly stated that Couture-Rouleau had been angry at the Canadian government for supporting the American offensive against ISIS in Iraq and Syria, and it led to him carrying out the attack which killed the soldier. Another friend of his revealed to Radio-Canada that he spent most of his time reading Jihadist literature and talked about dying as a martyr in Jihad.

Radio-Canada also obtained further information on this and discovered that Couture-Rouleau had convinced five of his close friends to convert to Islam. One of them stated that he was 'obsessed' with his new religion and was trying to get other people to follow him as well. A source also revealed that one of his friends was of the opinion that Couture-Rouleau was getting carried away by the extremist interpretation of the Koran that he found on the internet and would not stop in his mission.

One of his relatives informed the

RCMP about him after he had started to openly express terrorist inclinations. He had plans to join the ISIS and fight for them in Iraq. He was put under surveillance by the RCMP and was suspected of joining a terrorist organization after becoming radicalized upon converting to Islam.

***

The Conservative government in Canada at the time immediately categorized the attack as a terrorist incident. Minister for Public Safety, Steven Blaney, went on record to state that the attack clearly indicated links to 'terrorist ideology'.

Federal authorities also confirmed that the attacker was a radicalized individual who had been motivated by Islamist radicalization. A statement issued by the Prime Minister's office stated that the attacker had been on a surveillance list consisting of ninety Canadians on terrorist watch.

Stephen Harper, the Canadian Prime Minister at the time, also gave a statement later during which he said that Patrick Vincent had been an unfortunate victim of an act of terrorism and that radicalized individuals were trying to invoke terror within the country.

Other scholars and news analysts characterized Couture-Rouleau as a terrorist and warned that the West could be seeing a lot more of these in the future.

Parliament Hill Shooting, Canada

On October 22, 2014, two days after the Saint-Jean-sur-Richelieu ramming attack, a series of shootings occurred at the Parliament Hill in Ottawa, Canada. Michael Zehaf-Bibeau went into the Canadian National War Memorial and fatally shot a soldier on ceremonial sentry duty. [33]

Michael Zehaf-Bibeau

257

He then went on to the nearby parliament building and inside the Centre Block where many Parliamentarians of Canada were in attendance. The members of Parliament had been attending caucuses when Zehaf-Bibeau tried to run inside and was shot down. He was involved in a shootout with security personnel before six officers opened fire at him and shot him thirty-one times.

Zehaf-Bibeau was seen entering the National War Museum with a rifle and a scarf covering his lower face. He went on toward Corporal Nathan Cirillo, one of the three sentries of the Ceremonial Guard. He was posted at the Tomb of the Unknown Soldier and, like all the others standing sentry at the memorial, was carrying an unloaded firearm. He was fatally shot at close range by Zehaf-Bibeau.

He reportedly yelled "For Iraq" before getting in his vehicle and driving over to the Parliament Hill. Cirillo was taken to the hospital.

Zehaf-Bibeau tried to go inside the Centre Block from under the Peace Tower entrance but was spotted by Samearn Son, a security guard on duty. Son saw the rifle and rushed to stop him. He was shot in the leg and eventually was unable to hold on to the attacker.

Zehaf-Bibeau was involved in a shootout with the other security guard and was wounded. He managed to run to the Library of Parliament and along the corridors of the Hall of Honour. He was being pursued by RCMP officers when he passed the doors of the committee rooms where the respective political parties of Canada were conducting caucuses. In one of the rooms, Prime Minister Stephen Harper was also attending a meeting with his political party.

Zehaf-Bibeau hid in an alcove near the entrance of the Library of Parliament where he was cornered by RCMP officers who ordered him to surrender. The alcove was near the office of Kevin Vickers, Sergeant-at-Arms of the House of Commons and a noted police force officer. Vickers entered the alcove with a gun and fired at the attacker. Witnesses report that almost thirty shots were fired at Zehaf-Bibeau before the final one that killed him. RCMP Officer Curtis Barett, the leader of the tactical formation attacking Zehaf-Bibeau, fired at him in response to a shot by the perpetrator and ultimately killed him. [34]

During the shootout, one of the bullets penetrated the room where the Conservative Political Party, along with Stephen Harper, was holding its meeting. Harper had to hide in a closet while the MPs barricaded the door. The Parliament buildings went into lockdown and Harper was evacuated as soon as the attacker had been killed.

***

Zehaf-Bibeau had grown up in Ottawa and Montreal, among other areas of Eastern Canada. His mother was a French-Canadian from Montreal, Quebec, and was the deputy chairperson in a division of the Canadian Immigration and Refugee Board. His father hailed from Libya and had migrated to Montreal back in the day. He ran a Tripoli café in the city.

His parents were divorced, and he had spent most of his time in Montreal after that. Zehaf-Bibeau used to visit Libya and had reportedly fought in the Libyan Civil War, in 2011, as well. He moved to

Canada some time later and became a miner.

He was a habitual offender with a criminal record for a number of offences including drug possession, larceny and violations of parole. Born a Roman Catholic, Zehaf-Bibeau had converted to Islam in 2004 and since then had been attending different mosques. He had been displaying 'erratic behaviour' and was even expelled from a mosque in British Columbia. Some of the other people at the mosques believed that he was mentally ill.

According to his friends and family, he was looking to settle down in an Islamic country since he did not 'fit in' in Canada.

Occasionally, he had been known to express extremist Islamist views and even alarmed the staff at the vehicle registry office where he went to register the car he used in the attacks. The purchase of the vehicle never went through due to a problem in his identification documents.

***

Corporal Nathan Cirillo died after being fatally shot while Samearn Son was

261

injured.

A number of memorials were held for the fallen, including a concert that was attended by Prince Charles. The annual Remembrance Day memorial held at the National Museum also commemorated Cirillo and was attended by fifty thousand people.

Leaders from all over the world, including Queen Elizabeth and Barack Obama, offered their support to Canada and expressed solidarity with the country in this difficult time.

***

All of the above-mentioned incidents are just a few of the terrorist attacks in a long list that have been carried out over the last few years across the world. Many of these have been perpetrated by the lone-wolf, self-radicalized terrorists who claim to be doing it for a greater purpose. Almost all of them are inspired by the ideology of a terrorist network known for carrying out attacks and mass murder. Usually these individuals are young adults, disillusioned and alienated, who are lured through social media and promised a sense of purpose.

Social networks like Facebook and Twitter bring people together and encourage them to talk about a common cause. Freedom of speech and identity protection is also easy to avail through the internet, and this attracts such people who can vent out their frustrations without being targeted by authorities or the general public.

It is easier to run a recruitment program through social networks for these terrorist organizations. They target such individuals who appear disturbed and easy to manipulate, mostly the young people, and provide them with a sense of purpose. This wrongful sense of purpose is what ultimately leads to such people becoming self-radicalized terrorists and carrying out terrorist activities.

The ISIS has had quite the success with their social media recruiting. They have managed to lure a number of young girls and boys toward their organization and encouraged them to fight for them. The young girls volunteer to become 'Jihadi brides', leave their home countries and go off to Syria or Iraq. Young men have been putting up violent videos and messages in support of the terror group, with most of them fleeing off to Syria to join the movement.

Recruitment through social media has been going on for quite some time and has led to most governments and agencies introducing stricter regulations in order to identify any potential threats or erratic behavior that could result in terrorism.

The San Bernardino Shootings

It was the deadliest terrorist attack to occur in the United States since the September 11 incident. Fourteen people were killed when a mass shooting was carried out in San Bernardino, California, and twenty-two people were gravely wounded. [35]

Syed Rizwan Farook and Tashfeen Malik were the terrorists who executed the attack, a married couple living in Redlands. Both were from Pakistani descent but were US citizens and had been planning the attack for years before executing it.

After the shooting took place, they fled in a rented SUV. They were later pursued by police and killed in a shootout. On December 3, 2015, the FBI started a counter terrorism investigation and found that, even though they didn't join any terrorist organizations, they followed them closely and even pledged allegiance to one of them. On December 6, 2015, it was officially considered to be a terrorism act by President Barack Obama, who delivered a prime-time speech from the Oval Office.

James B. Comey, director of the FBI, explained that the perpetrators were actually "homegrown violent extremists" who were inspired by terrorist groups. However, they weren't directed by these groups and weren't a part of terrorist networks or groups. They had become radicalized throughout the years, taking in "poison from and on the internet" and continuously expressing their dedication to jihadism in messages they sent to each other. Throughout the years, they had been able to amass a significant amount of weapons and equipment to make ammunition and even bombs in their house.

Enrique Marquez Jr., the former neighbor of the couple, was investigated for his association with the attack when it was found that he had purchased two of the rifles used in the shooting. He was arrested on December 17, 2015, and was later charged with three federal counts.

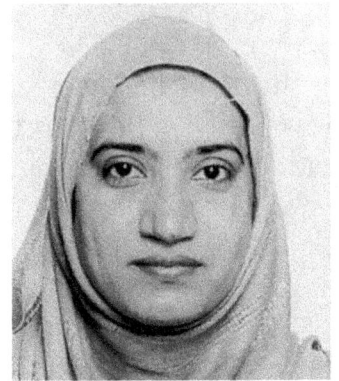
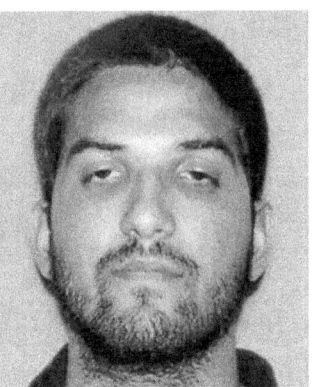

Syed Rizwan Farook and Tashfeen Malik

December 2, 2015, the perpetrators left their daughter with Farook's mother, telling her they were heading to a doctor's appointment. The mother had no idea what was going on and was not involved in the planning or the execution of the incident in any way. Farook, who was a health inspector, attended an event that day at the Inland Regional Center, and the event was already in place when the shooting started. There were about 80 people in attendance. Co-workers stated that Farook was really quiet that day and left in the middle of the event without explaining why. Reports from witnesses also state that he seemed agitated or angry when he left and didn't speak to anyone the whole time.

At 10:59 a.m., the couple armed themselves with pistols and rifles and opened fire on the attendees. They hid their faces using ski masks, wore black gear, and the entire shooting took about four minutes where almost 75 bullets were fired. They left the scene after the shooting took place, but witnesses were able to recognize Farook by his voice and body shape. Sources stated that Malik had pledged allegiance to ISIL's leader on a Facebook account she connected with before the attack took place where she announced that she believed in everything the group represents.

They left three explosive devices associated to one another at the Center after the shooting took place. They were pipe bombs connected with a car that was remote controlled. Luckily, the devices were poorly constructed and didn't explode. Police believe that the bombs were supposed to target police and emergency personnel coming to the scene, but they did not detonate.

Officials said that the two rifles used in the shooting were an AR-15 and a M-16. Witnesses said that there was one additional person in the shooting. The police later arrested a person who was running away on foot from the shootout with police.

***

It took about four minutes for police to reach the place of the shooting. Police got into the building using a battering ram, and the FBI, along with the LA Police, were called in to help. The explosive devices used were later on detonated. The U.S. Homeland Security Department sent a surveillance aircraft as well for assistance.

Police started looking for suspects. Witnesses gave police all the details related to Farook, where it was quickly learned that he had rented a black SUV four days before the shooting took place. During the pursuit, one fake explosive was thrown at police but it failed to detonate. After the police were able to stop the SUV, the couple started exchanging fire with police for about five minutes until they were both shot and killed. One of them died inside the car whereas the other died while trying to get out and escape.

***

Truck riddled with bullets

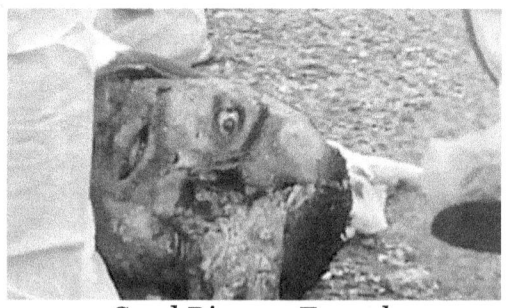

Syed Rizwan Farook

Shootout scene

Overall, fourteen civilians were killed and twenty-two were injured. It took about fifteen minutes to get them to the hospital. One of the injured was a police officer. The fourteen dead victims were 26 to 60 years old, eight being San Bernardino citizens and others from Riverside, L.A., and Orange counties. Most of them worked in the Center where the shooting took place and knew Farook. A vigil took place after the shooting to honor the victims where citizens and individuals from all over California gathered together and lit candles. This was the first time an event like this took place in San Bernardino, and it truly left everyone in shock.

***

Based on reports by the newspaper La Stampa, Farook's father stated that his son had Al Baghdadi's ideology and was hoping to establish an Islamic State and was obsessed with Israel. However, a spokesperson from CAIR then stated that his father didn't make these statements at all.

Two officials from the government explained that there weren't any red flags that he had traveled to Saudi Arabia for Hajj during 2013. Hajj is the yearly pilgrimage that thousands of Muslims participate in every year. Officials also stated that he was in Saudi Arabia for nine days in 2014.

Malik entered the U.S. on a K1 fiancée visa which required strict screening. Her application was completed during September 2014, and she was given a conditional green card in July. Getting this card would require them to prove that their marriage was real and they would have had to undergo three extensive and strict security and criminal screenings. Malik also went through two interviews, and no suspicious signs were found in all of her screening and interviewing process.

December 16, 2015, Director of the FBI James Comey explained that, based on the Bureau's investigation, there were physical meetings between both of them which led to marriage. There were also many personal messages between them which showed their dedication to martyrdom. Investigation also showed that both of them were continuously checking extremist information online and were radicalized even before they met on the establishment of ISIL.

Investigations by the FBI showed that the shooters were violent extremists who were mainly inspired by international terrorist organizations. They spent a year planning the attack, including enrolling in target practice and looking for places to take care of their child. In target practice, they focused on learning how to shoot heavy firearms that were similar to the ones they had used the day of the shooting. The FBI stated that there were also several telephonic conversations that took place between them and other wanted persons in FBI probes who were linked to terrorism and had the same exact terrorist ideology as the couple. They had also had contact with individuals from numerous terrorist groups such as Nusra Front, Al Shabaab, and even Al-Qaeda, who are all known for having extremist opinions and have been conducting terrorist acts for years.

In an Arabic language broadcast by ISIL, the terrorist group described the perpetrators as supporters and as the caliphate's soldiers. The large weapons stockpile used by the shooters indicated that there were more attacks planned in the future. Digital equipment found in their house suggested that they were planning a large attack after this one. The couple believed that by doing this, they were killing people who oppose their religion and this is what God ordered them to do. However, this is completely untrue as the Koran doesn't state that this is the way to achieve martyrdom.

Two weeks before the shooting took place, Farook took a $28,500 loan from the bank which was later on deposited to his bank account. There is a possibility that $10,000 were used to purchase the rifles used in the attack.

After the perpetrators' death, the search started in their house in Redlands, a couple of miles from San Bernardino. This is the first place where the couple met after the shooting took place and where they resided for years throughout their stay in the United States. On December 2, 2015, the police executed a search warrant and were going through the house. Police sent dogs and robots to search their home, and they found handgun rounds, caliber rounds, and explosive devices, all believed to have been planned to be used by the couple in later attacks after they fled the shooting scene. The FBI also recovered nineteen pipes of the types that could be changed into bombs if successfully used. The couple wasn't successful in hiding or destroying their electronics, such as their phones, computers, and hard drives before the attack took place. Pursuant to the warrant, police searched the house of Farook's brother and father; the latter were completely cooperative and weren't arrested.

On December 10, 2015, federal authorities started searching around Seccombe Lake after they received a tip that the perpetrators were in the area the day of the shooting. However, nothing relevant was found by divers. They also searched the brother's home, but he wasn't arrested or considered to be a suspect. Also, investigators and law enforcement received information that someone who looked like Farook tried to access an office tower in downtown L.A. a couple of weeks before the shooting took place. After looking at the information offered by the office's building management, the FBI concluded that this man had nothing to do with the attack or the events leading to it. However, they later found that the couple had an accomplice, Enrique Marquez Jr, who was helping them throughout the planning process and different events throughout the years.

Their neighbor Stacy Mozer explained that he saw neighbors carrying many boxes out of their house, possibly evidence, and that twelve agents were at the house. Shockingly, many of their neighbors explained how kind the couple were to them and how they would have never assumed that something like this would have been done by them, especially as they hadn't see any strange behavior during the past years.

***

Enrique Marquez, Jr.

Enrique Marquez was Farook's neighbor until May 2015 and was investigated in association with his purchase of the rifles used in this attack. However, there wasn't any record of Marquez providing the weapons to the shooters. Marquez regularly attended Islamic centers and converted to Islam during 2007. He was involved in a sham marriage for about $10,000 so Mariya Chernykh could get the green card and become a citizen of the United States.

In December 2015, law enforcement searched his house after obtaining a search warrant. He wasn't charged with any crime in the beginning and ended up waiving his Miranda rights and completely cooperated with the FBI. However, he was arrested at the end of December 2015 and charged with three different counts, also with immigration fraud and ''straw purchase'' associated charge.

Federal prosecutors claim that

during 2014, both Farook and Enrique planned to carry out attacks on Riverside's community college and on California State. The attack on California State would include a pipe bomb interrupting traffic, followed by one of them shooting at cars while the other one would shoot at emergency teams responding to the shooting. However, they weren't able to execute this plan when three men were arrested because they planned to kill U.S. citizens in Afghanistan. Both of them spent the next years in Farook's house, listening to and reading extremist Islamist propaganda, such as Inspire magazine, which is considered to be Al Qaeda's official publication.

A court hearing in Riverside ruled that Marquez should be held without bail, explaining that Marquez was dangerous to the community and people if released, especially that he greatly contributed to the shooting and that he wanted to implement a terrorist attack with Farook which would have resulted in significant losses to the country and people.

***

After the perpetrators' corpses [36] were released by police, none of the Islamic cemeteries would accept their remains, and it actually took a week to a find a cemetery to do that. The burial took place at an unannounced location away from San Bernardino. Based on two prominent mosque members, many of the Muslim community in San Bernardino forewent attending the funeral, which was only attended by ten people, including Farook's relatives. This proved that the Muslim community didn't agree in any way possible with the shooting that took place and the ideology behind it.

American Muslim organizations, such as CAIR and Orange County's Islamic society, condemned the shootings and explained that this doesn't represent the Islamic religion. A night vigil took place by the organizations in San Bernardino. After the shooting took place, the organization reported an increase in hate crimes against Muslims, including throwing the head of a pig at a mosque, assault on a shop owner, and the endless death threats. Various attacks and vandalism acts took place in South California after the attack, and

Muslims were being exposed to continuous hate.

The shooting also gained international and national attention. President Obama urged on the importance of implementing "common sense" firearm safety laws and stricter background checks to decrease the amount of shootings taking place in the country. Obama also called for new legislation to prevent individuals who are on the no-fly list from buying weapons. This was mainly due to the increase in the number of shootings taking place during the previous years, especially that some of them were related to terrorism whereas others were due to other problems, such as mental health. However, Paul Ryan objected to this proposal, explaining that this would violate the due process rights of these individuals.

Many Democrats tried to tighten gun control regulations after that, placing blame on the American culture that enables individuals who aren't even allowed to get on airplanes to easily purchase guns. Many of the California State's members proposed to discuss some firearm control proposals that were stalled before. After the San

Bernardino shooting, sales of firearms, especially in California, increased by 18,000, which was impressive considering the decrease in sales throughout the year before that.

On the other hand, Donald Trump, who is also the Republican presumptive nominee, called for a complete ban on individuals practicing Islam from entering the U.S. until the government is able to really understand what has happened. However, his statement then received backlash all over the world, even the White House, which said this would breach the U.S. Constitution. Many protesters explained that there are many Muslims who currently live in the U.S. who have never caused any issues, with many of them even serving in the military and army.

The attack started the debate of whether the U.S. government is going to expand their surveillance on Americans, and specifically if Congress is going to adopt new regulations mandating that companies, especially those in the technological sector, offer a back door so law enforcement can have encrypted data.

On February 9, 2016, the FBI announced that they were unable to access one of the phones they recovered, an iPhone 5C owned by one of the shooters, because of its developed security features. The FBI then asked Apple to create a new operating system for the phone that could be in the phone's access memory so certain security features can be disabled. However, Apple declined because of its rule to never weaken the product's security features. The FBI then insisted on their position by applying to a federal judge to issue a court order asking Apple to create the required software. Apple explained that this creation is going to pose a risk toward their other customers, because there is no absolute guarantee that this software is going to be accessed by someone else or not loaded again.

In response to Apple's position, the US Justice Department filed another application asking the federal court to direct the company to comply with their request. However, the new application explained that the company will install the software on its premises, and after the FBI is able to access the phone and retrieve the information they need, the company can them remove the malware and destroy it. Apple explained that it discussed with the FBI four techniques to be able to access the information they need in January, but one of the promising techniques was ruled out unintentionally while investigations were taking place.

After the phone was recovered, the FBI requested San Bernardino to reset the iCloud account's password to get the data they need. However, this led to the phone not being able to back up any data unless the password is successfully entered. This was later on confirmed by the U.S. Justice Department, which explained that any type of background would be insufficient as they wouldn't be able to recover the data they need from it. National reactions to the opposition and reaction from Apple to the order varied and were mixed.

On March 29, 2016, the FBI announced that they had purchased a tool to hack the phone, without Apples help. [37]

Final Thoughts

The Islamic terror threat has already changed our way of life. To see it for yourself, just go to any airport. As a terrorist group, ISIS poses a threat to North America. They have the ability to radicalize young Americans to conduct attacks here.

The FBI has over 1,000 open investigations into homegrown extremists, the vast majority radicalized by ISIS and a large number of which relate to individuals who may be plotting attacks here at home. Such attacks have already occurred in the U.S. and Canada. Others have been arrested before they could act.

While the sophistication of such homegrown attacks is likely to be fairly low, the potential exists for the quantity of these kinds of attacks to be large. The number of ISIS followers in the U.S. alone is in the thousands.

Thank you to our editor, proofreaders, and cover artist for your support:

~ RJ Parker & Peter Vronsky

Aeternum Designs (book cover)

Bettye McKee (editor)

Lorrie Suzanne Phillippe

Marlene Fabregas

Darlene Horn

Ron Steed

Lee Knieper Husemann

Katherine McCarthy

Robyn MacEachern

Linda H. Bergeron

Kathi Garcia

Amanda Martin

RJ Parker

RJ Parker, P.Mgr., MCrim, is an award-winning and bestselling true crime author and co-owner with his daughters of RJ Parker Publishing, Inc. He has written 20 true crime books, and have published over 80 books; available in eBook, paperback and audiobook editions, which have sold in over 100 countries. He holds certifications in Serial Crime and Criminal Profiling.

Parker was born and raised in Newfoundland and now resides in Ontario and Newfoundland, Canada. Parker started writing after becoming disabled with Anklyosing Spondylitis. He spent twenty-five years in various facets of Government and has two professional designations. In his spare time, RJ enjoys playing the guitar, mandolin, and piano. To date, RJ has donated over 3,000 autographed books to allied troops serving overseas and to our wounded warriors recovering in Naval and Army hospitals all over the world. He also donates a percentage of his royalties to Victims of Violent Crimes.

If you are a police officer, firefighter, paramedic or serve in the military, active or retired, RJ gives his eBooks freely in appreciation for your service.

Crimes Canada: True Crimes That Shocked The Nation is a collection of books by RJ Parker and Peter Vronsky.

Crimes Canada:

www.CrimesCanada.com

Author's Email:

AuthorRJParker@gmail.com

Publisher's Email:

Agent@RJParkerPublishing.com

Website:

http://m.RJPARKERPUBLISHING.com/

Twitter:

www.Twitter.com/AuthorRJParker

Facebook:

www.facebook.com/RJParkerPublishing

Amazon Author's Page:

http://rjpp.ca/RJ-PARKER-BOOKS

** SIGN UP FOR OUR MONTLY NEWSLETTER

Http://rjpp.ca/RJ-PARKER-NEWSLETTER **

Dr. Peter Vronsky, PhD

P**eter Vronsky** is a Bestselling Author, University Professor, Filmmaker and Investigative Historian. He is the author of two definitive bestselling books on the history and psychopathology of serial homicide, *Serial Killers: The Method and Madness of Monsters (2004)* and *Female Serial Killers: How and Why Women Become Monsters (2007).*

Vronsky is also a historian of espionage, insurgency and military history. His most recent book is *Ridgeway: The American Fenian Invasion and the Forgotten 1866 Battle that Made Canada (Penguin Books: 2011)* an investigative account of the hidden history of Canada's first modern battle and the Irish Fenian insurgency.

Vronsky contributed chapters in the *Annual True Crimes Serial Killers Collection; Volumes 1, 2 and 3.* by RJ Parker Publishing. Most recently, Peter and RJ formed VP Publications and produce the *Crimes Canada: True Crimes That Shocked The Nation* monthly book series. Peter and RJ have also collaborated on several books including;

Revenge Killings: The Story of LAPD Cop and Serial Killer Chris Dorner

Forensic Analysis in Criminal Investigations: COLD CASES SOLVED

Radical Islamic Terrorism in America Today (May 2016)

Vronsky holds a PhD from the University of Toronto in the fields of the history of espionage in international relations and criminal justice history. He currently lectures in history of the Third Reich, the American Civil War, history of terrorism, espionage and international relations in the 20th century at Ryerson University in Toronto.

Peter lives in Toronto and Venice, Italy. His contact information:

www.petervronsky.org
www.serialkillerchronicles.com
www.investigativehistory.com
www.ridgewaybattle.ca
www.fenians.org
Facebook
https://www.facebook.com/killersbypetervronsky/

eMail
info@PeterVronsky.com
editors@CrimesCanada.com

Introduction References

[1] Jason Burke, The New Threat: The Past, Present, and Future of Islamic Militancy, New York: The New Press, 2015.

[2] Charles Allen, God's Terrorists: The Wahhabi Cult and the Hidden Roots of Modern Jihad, New York: Da Capo Press, 2006.

[3] Karl Vick, "Violence at work tied to loss of esteem", St. Petersburg Times, Dec 17, 1993.

[4] Samuel P. Huntington, "The Clash of Civilizations?", Foreign Affairs, Summer 1993.

[5] James Barr, A Line in the Sand: The Anglo-French Struggle for the Middle East, 1914-1948, New York: Norton, 2012.

[6] Frank Viola, Pagan Christianity? Exploring the Roots of Our Church Practices, Carol Stream, IL:: Tyndale House Publishers, 2004.

[7] James Barr, Setting the Desert on Fire: T. E. Lawrence and Britain's Secret War in Arabia, 1916-1918, New York: WW Norton, 2008.

[8] James Barr, A Line in the Sand

[9] Benny Morris, Righteous Victims: A History of the Zionist-Arab Conflict, 1881-1998, New York: Vintage Random House, 2011.

[10] Stephen Kinzer, All the Shah's Men: An American Coup and the Roots of Middle East Terror, John Whiley & Sons, 2003.

[11] Steve Coll, Ghost Wars: The Secret History of the CIA, Afghanistan, and bin Laden, from the Soviet Invasion to September 10, 2001, New York:

Penguin Books, 2004.

[12] Jason Burke, Al-Qaeda: The True Story of Radical Islam, London: I. B. Tauris, 2004.

[13] See Gadhafi Speech to the United Nations General Assembly 23/9/2009, http://www.petervronsky.org/HIS590/gaddafi-speech.htm

[1] http://www.frontpagemag.com/fpm/258670/myth-muslim-radicalization-daniel-greenfield

[2] http://khaledhosseini.com/biography/

[3] https://en.wikipedia.org/wiki/Jihad

[4] http://www.theglobalist.com/islam-and-the-west-clash-of-civilizations/

[5] http://www.brookings.edu/~/media/research/files/papers/2015/03/ideology-of-islamic-state-bunzel/the-ideology-of-the-islamic-state.pdf

[6] http://www.pbs.org/wgbh/pages/frontline/shows/target/etc/modern.html

[7] http://www.theguardian.com/world/live/2015/nov/13/shootings-reported-in-eastern-paris-live

[8] http://www.bbc.com/news/world-asia-30491435

[9] http://www.cnn.com/2015/04/14/africa/nigeria-kidnapping-anniversary/

[10] http://globalnews.ca/news/1314505/how-boko-haram-kidnapped-hundreds-of-schoolgirls-from-chibok/

[11] http://mashable.com/2015/10/31/russian-plane-crash-egypt-cause/#nBojQ7JIY5qW

[12] http://www.cbc.ca/news/world/what-is-shariah-law-1.2674937

[13] http://www.telegraph.co.uk/news/worldnews/northamerica/usa/11450902/Boston-bombings-timeline-of-marathon-attack-and-trial-of-Dzhokhar-Tsarnaev.html

[14] http://swampland.time.com/2013/04/16/a-short-history-of-pressure-cooker-bombs/

[15] http://www.cbsnews.com/pictures/boston-marathon-bombing-victims/

[16] http://journalistsresource.org/studies/government/criminal-justice/boston-marathon-bombings-research-lessons

[17] http://info.publicintelligence.net/DHS-FBI-BostonMarathonDevices.pdf

[18] http://www.biography.com/people/dzhokhar-tsarnaev-21196765#synopsis

[19] http://en.citizendium.org/wiki/Self-radicalization

[20] https://www.bostonglobe.com/metro/2014/10/11/witnes

s-can-testify-that-bombing-suspect-tsarnaev-knew-brother-was-involved-waltham-triple-slaying-according-court-filing/dEFhb6pk9HrNC8XOXWMbYM/story.html

21 http://tech.mit.edu/V133/N19/policeman.html

22 http://www.nbcnews.com/storyline/boston-bombing-anniversary/too-many-guns-how-shootout-bombing-suspects-spiraled-chaos-n80236

23 http://ash.harvard.edu/files/why_was_boston_strong.pdf

24 http://emergency.cdc.gov/preparedness/shelter/

25 http://www.cpps.com/blog/wp-content/uploads/2010/08/Fort-Hood-Case-Study-FINAL.pdf

26 http://www.purpleheart.org/HistoryOrder.aspx

27 http://en.academic.ru/dic.nsf/enwiki/11679926

28 http://news.intelwire.com/2012/07/the-following-e-mails-between-maj.html

29 http://www.cbsnews.com/news/who-was-anwar-al-awlaki/

30 http://www.crimemuseum.org/crime-library/the-washington-dc-sniper

31 https://www.thestar.com/news/canada/2014/10/21/soldier_run_down_in_possible_quebec_terror_attack_dies.html

32 http://news.nationalpost.com/news/canada/patrice-vincent-killed-in-saint-jean-sur-richelieu-attack-was-a-distinguished-soldier-for-28-years-pm-says

33 http://www.macleans.ca/news/canada/michael-zehaf-bibeau-addict-drifter-walking-contradiction/

34 http://www.rcmp-grc.gc.ca/en/independent-investigation-death-michael-zehaf-bibeau

35 http://www.nytimes.com/interactive/2015/12/02/us/california-mass-shooting-san-bernardino.html?_r=0

36 http://www.ibtimes.com/san-bernardino-shooting-syed-rizwan-farook-tashfeen-malik-get-muslim-burials-fbi-2229577

37 http://money.cnn.com/2016/03/28/news/companies/fbi-apple-iphone-case-cracked/?iid=EL